200 cakes and bakes

D0532560

hamlyn | all colour cookbook

200 cakes and bakes

Sara Lewis

*For Miss Morley, an inspirational
teacher and lifelong friend*

An Hachette UK Company
www.hachette.co.uk

First published in Great Britain in 2008 by Hamlyn,
a division of Octopus Publishing Group Ltd
Endeavour House, 189 Shaftesbury Avenue
London WC2H 8JY
www.octopusbooks.co.uk

ISBN: 978-0-600-61730-3

A CIP catalogue record for this book is available
from the British Library

Printed and bound in China

5 6 7 8 9 10

Both metric and imperial measurements have been given
in all recipes. Use one set of measurements only, and not a
mixture of both.

Standard level spoon measurements are used in all recipes.
1 tablespoon = one 15 ml spoon
1 teaspoon = one 5 ml spoon

Ovens should be preheated to the specified temperature
– if using a fan-assisted oven, follow the manufacturer's
instructions for adjusting the time and the temperature.

Fresh herbs should be used unless otherwise stated.

Medium eggs should be used unless otherwise stated.

The Department of Health advises that eggs should not be
consumed raw. This book contains some dishes made with
raw or lightly cooked eggs. It is prudent for vulnerable
people such as pregnant and nursing mothers, invalids, the
elderly, babies and young children to avoid uncooked or
lightly cooked dishes made with eggs. Once prepared, these
dishes should be kept refrigerated and used promptly.

This book includes dishes made with nuts and nut
derivatives. It is advisable for those with known allergic
reactions to nuts and nut derivatives and those who may be
potentially vulnerable to these allergies, such as pregnant and
nursing mothers, invalids, the elderly, babies and children, to
avoid dishes made with nuts and nut oils. It is also prudent to
check the labels of pre-prepared ingredients for the possible
inclusion of nut derivatives.

contents

introduction

introduction

Making your own cakes and biscuits is immensely rewarding and relaxing. After a hectic week, making up a batch of cookies can be a great therapeutic way to unwind. The wonderful smell of their baking will soon have the family gravitating towards the kitchen, clamouring to eat them before they have had an opportunity to go cold.

Homemade cakes and bakes surpass any shop-bought version, no matter how expensive, and are a highly personal way to spoil family and friends. Many of the centrepiece cakes (see pages 134–179), for example, can be adapted for a special birthday with the addition of candles and perhaps a piped chocolate or iced message. Or why not take a batch of homemade small cakes (see pages 14–63) or cookies (see pages 64–107) when visiting friends, instead of a bunch of flowers. If you don't have much time then try the traybakes (see pages 108–133). They are all quick and

easy to assemble and are perfect for taking on picnics or packing into school or office lunchboxes. Many of the cakes can also be served warm so that they double as a pudding when served with custard or ice cream.

With many children no longer doing cookery at school, baking is also a good way of encouraging children to learn to cook. There is no mystique to cake baking and it really isn't as tricky as some people think. Providing you have a good set of scales and some basic cake tins and you follow the recipes accurately, then it really is child's play. In addition, you know exactly what has gone into your own cooking so you can keep artificial flavourings and additives to a minimum. You probably already have many of the ingredients in your store cupboard, and any specialist ingredients can be added to the trolley next time you are in the supermarket.

baking equipment

The recipes in this book are all easy to make and the chances are you will already have most of the basic equipment needed to make them. Any additional items can be bought in your nearest supermarket superstore, high street department store or hardware store.

scales

Good measuring scales are absolutely essential for cake making. Too much fat and the cake will sink, too much flour and the cake will be dry. Digital add-and-weigh scales are the easiest and clearest to use as the amount is shown with pinpoint accuracy.

Unlike the more traditional balance scales, you can place your usual mixing bowl on top, press the control button to zero then add and measure out your chosen ingredients. Reset the scales to zero and you can add more ingredients to the same bowl – ideal when weighing out butter and sugar for a creamed cake or flour, sugar and butter for a rubbed-in cake.

A conversion button means you can choose to use either metric or imperial measurements, although it is crucial that you use just one set of measurements for an entire recipe. Add-and-weigh scales also tend to be more compact than balance scales. The disadvantage is that the battery will run out at some point, so keep a spare handy.

If choosing spring-balanced scales make sure the small amounts are easy to read, some scales have indicator lines that go up only in 50 g (2 oz) increments.

Use an unopened packet of butter to double-check that your scales are accurate. The amount shown should match that on the butter packet. If not, adjust them until they do.

measuring spoons

A set of measuring spoons – from ¼ teaspoon up to 1 tablespoon – are invaluable for measuring out ingredients such as spices, baking powder, lemon juice, vanilla essence and oil. When measuring out dry ingredients, all spoonfuls should be level unless otherwise stated in the recipe.

measuring jug

A glass measuring jug tends to be easier to read and longer lasting than a plastic one, providing you don't drop it on the kitchen floor! Stand it on a flat surface and bend down to read the measurement rather than hold it up to eye level.

mixing bowls

These can be of plain glass, stainless steel, china or plastic. You will need a minimum of three in decreasing sizes, so that they fit inside each other for easy storage.

If you like to make large fruit cakes or celebration cakes, then an extra large mixing bowl may be useful as well.

cooling rack

Once baked, cakes and cookies need to be transferred to a wire rack so that the steam can escape and the bases stay dry. Choose one with narrow gaps between the wires or improvise and use the grill rack instead.

biscuit cutters

A good-quality set of plain and fluted round metal biscuit cutters will last a lifetime and can be used not only for cookies but also when making little tarts, pies and scones.

piping bag and tubes

These are not essential but are good for piping meringues, éclairs and biscuit mixture. It's useful to have a large 1 cm (½ inch) fluted tube and a plain tube. Nylon piping bags tend to be more flexible and easier to use than the thicker plastic ones.

food processor versus electric whisk

Both pieces of equipment are extremely useful for effortlessly making creamed and rubbed-in cakes, cookies, scones and frostings. Because a food processor has a lid there is less mess and it can contain that inevitable fine mist of icing sugar or flour. When adding fruit, remember to swap the blade from the metal to the plastic one and to blitz for the shortest time possible so that the fruit is mixed in rather than chopped.

Both a hand-held and a free-standing electric mixer are ideal for whisking, although only a hand-held electric mixer can be used for whisking ingredients in a bowl over a saucepan of simmering water.

additional useful equipment

- **Pastry brush** – for greasing cake tins and glazing tops of scones.
- **Flexible plastic spatula** – perfect for folding in flour or whisked egg whites and for scooping cake mixture into cake tins.
- **Palette knife** – a small, 10 cm (4 inch), one is ideal for loosening cakes while still in their tins. A larger, 25 cm (10 inch), one is good for transferring a larger cake from a cooling rack to a serving plate.
- **Rolling pin** – you probably already have one, but if buying for the first time, choose one without handles.
- **Balloon whisk** – for beating frostings and whipping cream.
- **Wooden spoon** – for mixing creamed and melted-method cakes. Choose one with a shorter handle for easy mixing.
- **Long thin metal skewer** – for checking whether the centre of the cake is cooked.

preparing cake tins

Grease your cake tin by brushing on a little sunflower or vegetable oil, using a pastry brush, or by smearing a small knob of butter thinly over the inside of the tin. Even nonstick tins need a light greasing before use unless fully lined with nonstick baking paper.

greaseproof paper versus nonstick baking paper

Nonstick baking paper, as the name suggests, is nonstick and can be used to line tins or baking sheets without the addition of any oil or butter. Greaseproof paper must always be greased after shaping and pressing into a greased tin. It is usually easiest to brush it lightly with a little oil.

Nonstick baking paper is preferable when lining baking sheets for meringues, roasting tins or deep round or square tins, where the base and side are lined.

how to line a...

Deep round cake tin Draw around the tin on nonstick baking paper and cut out the circle. Cut a strip of paper a little taller than the tin sides and a little longer so that the paper overlaps when in the tin. Fold up a strip along the bottom edge then snip into it at intervals. Stand the paper inside the ungreased tin with the snipped edge on the base of the tin. Place the paper circle on top of this.

Deep square cake tin This technique is similar, but instead of snipping all around the bottom edge of the vertical lining paper, make cuts only where the paper will fit into the corners of the tin.

Sandwich tin Draw around the tin on greaseproof paper and cut out the circle. Press into the base of the greased tin then grease the paper.

Roasting tin or Swiss roll tin Cut a rectangle of nonstick baking paper larger than the top of the tin. Make diagonal cuts into the corners then press the paper into the base of the ungreased tin, so that the base and sides of the tin are lined and, for a Swiss roll tin, the paper stands a little above the tin's sides.

Loaf tin Press a strip of greaseproof paper the same length as the longest side, and wide enough to cover the base and up the two long sides, into a greased tin then grease the paper. You don't need to line the short ends of the tin.

baking know-how

Cooking times are always a guide so do check on your cake's progress during cooking. Rely only on the oven's glass door if possible. Certainly, never open the door until just over halfway through cooking, when the cake will be set and at less risk of sinking. Even then, open it very slightly, just enough to see how the cake is doing. If it is cooking more quickly at the front or sides, rotate the cake so it cooks evenly.

Cakes should be an even colour all over when cooked. Sponge cakes will spring back when gently pressed with fingertips. A fine skewer pushed into the middle of larger cakes should come out clean and dry.

Make sure you select the correct size tin for your cake. Tins should be measured across the base, especially if you are using a roasting dish as these normally have slightly sloping sides and a lip on the top edge.

troubleshooting

If your cake doesn't turn out as expected see if you can identify the problem from the following.

Cake cracks heavily on top
• Cake cooked at too high a temperature or on too high an oven shelf.
• Rounded rather than level teaspoons of raising agent were used.
• Too small a cake tin was used so cake is very deep.

Fruit sinks
• Too much fruit for the cake mixture too hold.
• Fruit was damp, or glacé cherries, if using, were very sticky with sugar.

Cake sinks
• Oven door was opened before the cake had set.
• Cake removed from oven before it was cooked right through.
• Too much raising agent so cake rose quickly but then collapsed before mixture was set.

Cake does not rise properly
• Air was knocked out — perhaps the flour was stirred into a whisked cake rather than being gently folded in.
• Oven at too low a temperature or was accidentally turned off.
• Raising agent such as baking powder was forgotten.
• Plain flour used in place of self-raising flour.
• Cake cooked in too large a tin.

Cake is dry

• Not enough fat.
• Cake was overcooked.
• Not wrapped and stored in a cake tin or plastic container after baking.

storing cakes

Cakes or cookies are generally best kept in an airtight container and stored in a cool place, but store cakes with cream or cream cheese fillings or frostings in the fridge. Most cakes freeze well although it's best to freeze those with glacé icing or fresh fruits unfilled or uniced. For very fragile cakes open freeze until firm then wrap in clingfilm or foil or pack into a plastic container. More robust cakes can be wrapped and then frozen. Large cakes can be sliced before freezing, and the slices interleaved with pieces of nonstick baking paper, so that just one or two slices can be thawed as required.

Use all frozen cakes within 3 months, defrost at room temperature for 2–4 hours depending on their size. Scones and cookies are best refreshed in the oven once they are defrosted, for 5–10 minutes at 180°C (350°F), Gas Mark 4.

don't forget to...

• **Use a pastry brush,** for greasing cake tins and glazing tops of scones.
• **Preheat the oven,** reducing the temperature by 10–20°C (18–36°F) if using a fan-assisted oven.
• **Centre the oven shelf,** unless you plan to cook more than one baking sheet at a time.
• **Grease and line the cake tins** before you start.
• **Use metric** *or* **imperial measurements,** not a mixture of the two.
• **Use level measuring spoons.**
• **Use a timer** so that you know when to check on the cake's progress.

little cakes

pistachio & chocolate meringues

Makes **16**
Preparation time **30 minutes**
Cooking time **45–60 minutes**

3 **egg whites**
175 g (6 oz) **caster sugar**
50 g (2 oz) **shelled pistachio nuts**, finely chopped
150 g (5 oz) **plain dark chocolate**, broken into pieces
150 ml (¼ pint) **double cream**

Whisk the egg whites in a large clean bowl until stiff. Gradually whisk in the sugar, a teaspoonful at a time, until it has all been added. Whisk for a few minutes more until the meringue mixture is thick and glossy.

Fold in the pistachios then spoon heaped teaspoonfuls of the mixture into rough swirly mounds on 2 large baking sheets lined with nonstick baking paper.

Bake in a preheated oven, 110°C (225°F), Gas Mark ¼, for 45–60 minutes or until the meringues are firm and may be easily peeled off the paper. Leave to cool still on the paper.

Melt the chocolate in a heatproof bowl set over a saucepan of gently simmering water. Lift the meringues off the paper and dip the bases into the chocolate. Return to the paper, tilted on their sides and leave in a cool place until the chocolate has hardened.

To serve, whip the cream until just holding its shape then use to sandwich the meringues together in pairs. Arrange in paper cake cases, if liked, on a cake plate or stand. Eat on the day they are filled. (Left plain, the meringues will keep for 2–3 days.)

For saffron & chocolate meringues, add a large pinch of saffron threads to the egg whites when first whisking them and omit the pistachios. Dip the meringues in the melted chocolate, fill with the whipped cream and serve as above.

easter cupcakes

Makes **12**
Preparation time **20 minutes,
 plus setting**
Cooking time **15–18 minutes**

125 g (4 oz) **plain flour**
125 g (4 oz) **caster sugar**
125 g (4 oz) **soft margarine**
1½ teaspoons **baking powder**
1½ teaspoons **vanilla essence**
2 **eggs**

For the topping
125 g (4 oz) **icing sugar,**
 sifted
½ teaspoon **vanilla essence**
4 teaspoons **water**
a few drops of **yellow, green
 and pink food colouring**
jelly beans, to decorate

Put all the cupcake ingredients in a mixing bowl or a food processor and beat until smooth. Spoon the mixture into foil cake cases arranged in a greased 12-hole deep muffin tin. Bake in a preheated oven, 180°C (350°F), Gas Mark 4, for 15–18 minutes until well risen and the cakes spring back when gently pressed with a fingertip. Leave to cool in the tin.

Make the topping. Mix together the icing sugar, vanilla and enough of the water to make a smooth icing. Divide the icing among 3 bowls and colour each batch differently. Turn the cakes out of the tin, ice them and decorate with jelly beans. Leave for 30 minutes for the icing to set.

For girly cupcakes, make the cupcakes as above but use just a few drops of pink food colouring to colour the icing and decorate the top of each cupcake with a single pastel-coloured sugared flower instead of the jelly beans.

lemon & orange drizzle cakes

Makes **12**
Preparation time **20 minutes**
Cooking time **12–15 minutes**

250 g (8 oz) **self-raising flour**
200 g (7 oz) **caster sugar**
grated rind and juice of
  1 **lemon**
grated rind and juice of
  1 **orange**
3 **eggs**
2 tablespoons **milk**
100 g (3½ oz) **butter**, melted

Put the flour in a mixing bowl then add half the sugar and half the lemon and orange rind. Lightly beat the eggs and milk together then add to the bowl with the melted butter. Beat together until just smooth.

Spoon the mixture into the sections of a greased 12-hole deep muffin tin. Bake in a preheated oven, 190°C (375°F), Gas Mark 5, for 12–15 minutes until well risen and the tops are craggy and firm to the touch.

Make the lemon and orange syrup. Put the remaining sugar and grated citrus rind in a bowl. Strain in the fruit juices then mix together until the sugar has just dissolved.

As soon as the cakes come out of the oven, loosen the edges and turn out. Arrange in a shallow dish, prick the tops with a fine skewer or fork and drizzle the syrup over, little by little, until absorbed by the cakes. Leave to cool. The cakes are best served on the day they are made.

For lemon syrup cakes, make up the mixture with 2 lemons and bake as above, finishing with a lemon-only syrup. Serve warm with vanilla ice cream for a delicious dessert.

orange & sultana scones

Makes **10**
Preparation time **20 minutes**
Cooking time **10 minutes**

375 g (12 oz) **self-raising flour**
50 g (2 oz) **butter**, diced
50 g (2 oz) **caster sugar**, plus extra for sprinkling
75 g (3 oz) **sultanas**
grated rind of **1 orange**
1 **egg**, beaten
150–200 ml (5–7 fl oz) **semi-skimmed milk**

To serve
5 tablespoons **apricot jam**
2 x 113 g (3¾ oz) packets **clotted cream**

Put the flour in a mixing bowl or a food processor. Add the butter and rub in with your fingertips or process until the mixture resembles fine breadcrumbs. Stir in the sugar, sultanas and orange rind.

Add all but 1 tablespoon of the egg then gradually mix in enough of the milk to mix to a soft but not sticky dough.

Knead lightly then roll out on a lightly floured surface until 1.5 cm (¾ inch) thick. Stamp out 5.5 cm (2¼ inch) circles using a plain round biscuit cutter. (Don't be tempted to roll out the dough thinner and make more scones as they will just look mean and miserly.) Transfer to a lightly greased baking sheet. Reknead the trimmings and continue rolling and stamping out until you have made 10 scones.

Brush the tops with the reserved egg and sprinkle lightly with a little extra caster sugar. Bake in a preheated oven, 200°C (400°F), Gas Mark 6, for 10–12 minutes until well risen and the tops are golden. Leave to cool on the baking sheet.

Serve the scones warm or just cold, split and filled with jam and clotted cream. They are best eaten on the day they are made.

For fat rascals, make the scones as above but omit the orange rind and sultanas and stir in ½ teaspoon ground cinnamon instead. Sprinkle the tops of the scones with 2 tablespoons caster sugar mixed with ½ teaspoon ground cinnamon before baking as above.

maple & pecan muffins

Makes **8**
Preparation time **10 minutes**
Cooking time **20–25 minutes**

300 g (10 oz) **self-raising flour**
1 teaspoon **baking powder**
125 g (4 oz) **soft brown sugar**
1 **egg**
50 ml (2 fl oz) **maple syrup**
250 ml (8 fl oz) **milk**
50 g (2 oz) **unsalted butter**, melted
125 g (4 oz) **white chocolate**, finely chopped
75 g (3 oz) **pecan nuts**, coarsely chopped

To decorate
chopped **pecans**
chopped **white chocolate**

Sift the flour and baking powder into a mixing bowl and stir in the sugar. Beat together the egg, maple syrup, milk and melted butter and beat into the dry ingredients until mixed. Fold in the chocolate and pecan nuts.

Divide the mixture evenly among 8 paper cake cases arranged in a 12-hole deep muffin tin and top with some extra chopped nuts and chocolate. Bake in a preheated oven, 200°C (400°F), Gas Mark 6, for 20–25 minutes until risen and golden. Transfer to a wire rack to cool.

For milk chocolate & walnut muffins, make the muffins as above but replace the white chocolate with 125 g (4 oz) finely chopped milk chocolate and the pecan nuts with 75 g (3 oz) coarsely chopped walnuts.

fruited griddle cakes

Makes **30**
Preparation time **25 minutes**
Cooking time **18 minutes**

250 g (8 oz) **self-raising flour**
125 g (4 oz) **butter**, diced
100 g (3½ oz) **caster sugar**,
  plus extra for sprinkling
50 g (2 oz) **currants**
50 g (2 oz) **sultanas**
1 teaspoon **ground mixed
  spice**
grated rind of ½ **lemon**
1 **egg**, beaten
1 tablespoon **milk**, if needed
oil, for greasing

Put the flour in a mixing bowl or a food processor. Add the butter and rub in with your fingertips or process until the mixture resembles fine breadcrumbs. Stir in the sugar, dried fruit, spice and lemon rind.

Add the egg then gradually mix in milk, if needed, to make a smooth dough. Knead lightly then roll out on a lightly floured surface until 5 mm (¼ inch) thick. Stamp out 5 cm (2 inch) circles using a fluted round biscuit cutter. Reknead the trimmings and continue rolling and stamping out until all the dough has been used.

Pour a little oil on to a piece of folded kitchen paper and use to grease a griddle or heavy nonstick frying pan. Heat the pan then add the cakes in batches, regreasing the griddle or pan as needed, and fry over a medium to low heat for about 3 minutes each side until golden brown and cooked through. Serve warm, sprinkled with a little extra sugar or spread with butter, if liked. Store in an airtight tin for up to 2 days.

For orange & cinnamon griddle cakes, use the grated rind of ½ orange instead of the lemon, and 1 teaspoon ground cinnamon in place of the mixed spice. Continue the recipe as above.

hot cross buns

Makes **12**
Preparation time **1 hour,**
  plus standing and rising
Cooking time **20 minutes**

2 tablespoons **active dried
  yeast**
1 teaspoon **sugar**
150 ml (¼ pint) **milk**, warmed
4 tablespoons warm **water**
500 g (1 lb) **strong bread
  flour**
1 teaspoon **salt**
½ teaspoon **ground mixed
  spice**
½ teaspoon **ground cinnamon**
½ teaspoon **grated nutmeg**
50 g (2 oz) **caster sugar**
50 g (2 oz) **butter**, melted and
  cooled
1 **egg**, beaten
125 g (4 oz) **currants**
40 g (1½ oz) **chopped mixed
  peel**
75 g (3 oz) **ready-made
  shortcrust pastry**

For the glaze
3 tablespoons **caster sugar**
4 tablespoons **milk and water**

Blend the yeast and sugar into the warmed milk and water. Stir into 125 g (4 oz) of the flour and leave in a warm place for about 20 minutes. Sift the remaining flour into a bowl, add the salt, spices and caster sugar.

Add the butter and egg to the yeast mixture. Stir this into the flour and mix well. Add the dried fruit and mix to a fairly soft dough. Add a little water if necessary.

Turn out the dough on to a lightly floured surface and knead well. Place in an oiled plastic bag and allow to rise for 1–1½ hours at room temperature until doubled in size. Turn out on to a floured surface and knead with your knuckles to knock out the air bubbles.

Divide the dough and shape into 12 round buns. Flatten each slightly then space well apart on floured baking sheets. Cover and put in a warm place again to rise for 20–30 minutes until doubled in size. Meanwhile, thinly roll out the pastry and cut it into 24 thin strips about 8 cm (3½ inches) long.

Dampen the strips and lay 2, damp side down, in a cross over each bun. Bake in a preheated oven, 190°C (375°F), Gas Mark 5, for 20 minutes or until golden brown and firm.

Make the glaze. Dissolve the sugar in the milk and water mixture over a low heat. Brush the cooked buns twice with the glaze, then serve hot, split and buttered.

For gingered fruit buns, use 125 g (4 oz) luxury dried fruit instead of the currants, and 2 tablespoons chopped glacé ginger in place of the mixed peel. Omit the pastry crosses and glaze as above.

churros

Makes **12**
Preparation time **20 minutes**
Cooking time **6–9 minutes**

200 g (7 oz) **plain flour**
¼ teaspoon **salt**
5 tablespoons **caster sugar**
275 ml (9 fl oz) **water**
1 **egg**, beaten
1 **egg yolk**
1 teaspoon **vanilla essence**
1 litre (1¾ pints) **sunflower oil**
1 teaspoon **ground cinnamon**

Mix the flour, salt and 1 tablespoon of the sugar in a bowl. Pour the water into a saucepan and bring to the boil. Take off the heat, add the flour mixture and beat well. Then return to the heat and stir until it forms a smooth ball that leaves the sides of the pan almost clean. Remove from the heat and leave to cool for 10 minutes.

Gradually beat the whole egg, egg yolk then the vanilla into the flour mixture until smooth. Spoon into a large nylon piping bag fitted with a 1 cm (½ inch) wide plain tube.

Pour the oil into a medium-sized saucepan to a depth of 2.5 cm (1 inch). Heat to 170°C (340°F) on a sugar thermometer or pipe a tiny amount of the mixture into the oil. If the oil bubbles instantly it is ready to use. Pipe coils, S-shapes and squiggly lines into the oil, in small batches, cutting the ends off with kitchen scissors. Cook the churros for 2–3 minutes until they float and are golden, turning over if needed to brown evenly.

Lift the churros out of the oil, drain well on kitchen paper then sprinkle with the remaining sugar mixed with the cinnamon. Continue piping and frying until all the mixture has been used. Serve warm or cold. They are best eaten on the day they are made.

For orange churros, add the grated rind of 1 orange and omit the vanilla essence. Continue as above. Sprinkle with plain caster sugar when cooked.

snow-covered ginger muffins

Makes **12**
Preparation time **30 minutes,**
  plus setting
Cooking time **10–15 minutes**

125 g (4 oz) **butter**
125 ml (4 fl oz) **maple syrup**
125 g (4 oz) **light muscovado**
  sugar
225 g (7½ oz) **self-raising**
  flour
1 teaspoon **baking powder**
1 teaspoon **ground ginger**
2 **eggs**
125 ml (4 fl oz) **milk**
3 tablespoons **glacé ginger,**
  chopped, plus extra to
  decorate

For the icing
200 g (7 oz) **icing sugar**
5–6 teaspoons **water**
2 pieces **glacé ginger**, sliced

Put the butter, syrup and sugar in a saucepan and heat gently, stirring until the butter has melted. Mix the flour, baking powder and ground ginger in a bowl. Beat the eggs and milk in another bowl.

Remove the butter saucepan from the heat, then beat in the flour mixture. Gradually beat in the egg and milk mixture, then stir in the chopped glacé ginger.

Divide the mixture evenly among paper cake cases arranged in a 12-hole deep muffin tin and bake in a preheated oven, 180°C (350°F), Gas Mark 4, for 10–15 minutes until well risen and cracked. Leave to cool in the tin.

Make the icing. Sift the icing sugar into a bowl and gradually mix in the water to create a smooth spoonable icing. Drizzle random lines of icing from a spoon over the muffins and complete with slices of glacé ginger. Leave the icing to harden for 30 minutes before serving.

For cinnamon & orange muffins, replace the ground ginger with 1 teaspoon ground cinnamon and use the grated rind of ½ orange instead of the glacé ginger. In the icing, replace the water with 4–5 teaspoons orange juice and decorate with a little extra grated orange rind.

viennese whirls

Makes **8**
Preparation time **20 minutes**
Cooking time **15 minutes**

100 g (3½ oz) **butter**,
    at room temperature
50 g (2 oz) **icing sugar**
2 **egg yolks**
½ teaspoon **vanilla essence**
125 g (4 oz) **self-raising flour**
25 g (1 oz) **cornflour**
10 frozen **raspberries**
1 tablespoon **strawberry or
    seedless raspberry jam**
sifted **icing sugar**,
    for dusting

Beat the butter and sugar together in a mixing bowl until pale and creamy. Gradually beat in the egg yolks and the vanilla then gradually beat in the flours until smooth.

Spoon the mixture into a large nylon piping bag fitted with a large star tube. Pipe double thickness circles of the mixture into 8 paper cake cases arranged in a 12-hole shallow bun tray. Press a still frozen raspberry in the centre of each.

Bake in a preheated oven, 180°C (350°F), Gas Mark 4, for about 15 minutes until pale golden. Leave to cool in the tin then add tiny spoonfuls of jam to the centre of each cake and dust lightly with sifted icing sugar. Transfer to a serving plate. These are best eaten on the day they are made.

For jumblies, pipe S-shapes of the above mixture on to greased baking sheets. Decorate with hundreds and thousands or sugar sprinkles and bake as above for 6–8 minutes until pale golden.

blueberry & lemon muffins

Makes **12**
Preparation time **15 minutes**
Cooking time **18–20 minutes**

175 g (6 oz) **malthouse or granary flour**
125 g (4 oz) **plain flour**
3 teaspoons **baking powder**
125 g (4 oz) **light muscovado sugar**
200 g (7 oz) **blueberries**
grated rind and juice of 1 **lemon**
4 tablespoons **olive or sunflower oil**
50 g (2 oz) **margarine or butter**, melted
3 **eggs**, beaten
150 ml (¼ pint) **semi-skimmed milk**

For the lemon frosting
125 g (4 oz) **icing sugar**
juice of ½ **lemon**

Mix the flours, baking powder, sugar and blueberries together in a mixing bowl. Put the remaining ingredients in a jug and fork together. Add to the dry ingredients and mix briefly with a fork.

Divide the mixture evenly among paper cake cases arranged in a 12-hole deep muffin tin. Bake in a preheated oven, 190°C (375°F), Gas Mark 5, for 18–20 minutes until well risen and the tops are cracked. Leave to cool in the tin for 15 minutes.

Make the frosting. Sift the icing sugar into a bowl and gradually mix in enough lemon juice to make a thin spoonable icing. Take the muffins out of the tin and drizzle icing from a spoon in random lines over the top. Leave to harden slightly and serve the muffins while still warm.

For raspberry & white chocolate muffins, replace the blueberries with the same weight of fresh raspberries. Bake as above then drizzle with 125 g (4 oz) melted white chocolate instead of the lemon frosting, sprinkling with a little grated white chocolate, if liked.

mini cappuccino cakes

Makes **12**
Preparation time **30 minutes**
Cooking time **12–14 minutes**

3 teaspoons **instant coffee**
2 teaspoons **boiling water**
175 g (6 oz) **soft margarine**
175 g (6 oz) **light muscovado sugar**
175 g (6 oz) **self-raising flour**
½ teaspoon **baking powder**
3 **eggs**

To decorate
300 ml (½ pint) **double cream**
75 g (3 oz) **dark or white chocolate curls**

Dissolve the coffee in the boiling water.

Beat the remaining cake ingredients in a mixing bowl or a food processor until smooth. Stir in the dissolved coffee. Divide the mixture evenly among the greased and base-lined sections of a 12-hole deep muffin tin and spread the surfaces level.

Bake in a preheated oven, 180°C (350°F), Gas Mark 4, for 12–14 minutes until well risen and the cakes spring back when gently pressed with a fingertip. Leave to cool in the tin for 5 minutes then loosen the edges, turn out on to a wire rack and peel off the lining paper. Leave to cool completely.

Turn each cake the right way up then slice in half horizontally. Whip the cream until softly peaking then use to sandwich the cakes together in pairs and spread the remainder on the tops. Sprinkle with the chocolate curls. These are best eaten on the day they are made.

For mini victoria sandwich cakes, omit the dissolved coffee and add 1 teaspoon vanilla essence to the cake mixture. Fill the baked cakes with a layer of strawberry jam and 150 ml (¼ pint) whipped double cream. Dust the tops with sifted icing sugar.

lamingtons

Makes **24**
Preparation time **20 minutes,
plus overnight standing**
Cooking time **25–30 minutes**

125 g (4 oz) **unsalted butter**,
   at room temperature
125 g (4 oz) **caster sugar**
2 **eggs**, lightly beaten
250 g (8 oz) **self-raising flour**
pinch of **salt**
4 tablespoons **milk**
1 teaspoon **vanilla extract**

For the icing
400 g (13 oz) **icing sugar**
100 g (3½ oz) **cocoa powder**
150–175 ml (5–6 fl oz)
   boiling water
200 g (7 oz) **desiccated
   coconut**

Beat the butter and sugar together in a mixing bowl until pale and creamy. Beat in the eggs, a little at a time, until incorporated. Sift in the flour and salt and fold into the creamed mixture with the milk and vanilla. Alternatively, beat all the cake ingredients together in a food processor until smooth.

Transfer the mixture to an oiled and base-lined 18 x 25 cm (7 x 10 inch) cake tin. Spread the surface level with a palette knife and bake in a preheated oven, 190°C (375°F), Gas Mark 5, for 25–30 minutes until risen and firm to the touch. Leave the cake to cool in the tin for 5 minutes then loosen the edges, turn out on to a wire rack and peel off the lining paper. Leave out overnight.

Make the icing. Sift the icing sugar and cocoa powder into a bowl, make a well in the centre and beat in the boiling water to make a smooth chocolate icing with a pouring consistency.

Cut the cooled cake into 24 pieces. Use 2 forks to dip each cake into the icing and then immediately coat with the coconut all over. Leave to set on baking paper.

For raspberry splits, when the cake is cool, cut it in half and sandwich back together with 6 tablespoons raspberry jam. Sift 200 g (7 oz) icing sugar into a bowl and mix in 5–6 teaspoons cold water to make a spreadable icing. Spread over the cake and decorate with sugar sprinkles. Leave to harden for 30 minutes, then cut into 24 squares.

chunky chocolate muffins

Makes **12**
Preparation time **20 minutes**
Cooking time **15–18 minutes**

275 g (9 oz) **plain flour**
25 g (1 oz) **cocoa powder**
3 teaspoons **baking powder**
150 g (5 oz) **caster sugar**
75 g (3 oz) **butter**, melted
3 **eggs**, beaten
150 ml (¼ pint) **milk**
1 teaspoon **vanilla essence**
200 g (7 oz) **white chocolate**,
  finely chopped
100 g (3½ oz) **plain dark or**
  milk chocolate, broken into
  pieces

Sift the flour, cocoa powder and baking powder into a mixing bowl. Add the sugar and stir together.

Add the melted butter, beaten eggs, milk and vanilla and fork together until almost mixed. Stir in the chopped white chocolate.

Spoon into paper cake cases arranged in a 12-hole deep muffin tin and bake in a preheated oven, 200°C (400°F), Gas Mark 6, for 18–20 minutes until well risen. Leave to cool in the tin for 5 minutes then transfer to a wire rack.

Melt the plain dark or milk chocolate in a heatproof bowl set over a saucepan of gently simmering water, then drizzle the chocolate in random lines over the top of each muffin.

Serve the muffins warm or cold. They are best eaten on the day they are made.

For white chocolate & cranberry muffins, soak 40 g (1½ oz) dried cranberries in 2 tablespoons boiling water for 10 minutes. Use 300 g (10 oz) plain flour instead of the mix of flour and cocoa powder. Continue the recipe above, adding the drained soaked cranberries along with the chopped white chocolate. Omit the melted chocolate topping and dust with a little sifted icing sugar to serve.

banana & sultana drop scones

Makes **10**
Preparation time **10 minutes**
Cooking time **8 minutes**

125 g (4 oz) **self-raising flour**
2 tablespoons **caster sugar**
½ teaspoon **baking powder**
1 small ripe **banana**, about
   125 g (4 oz) with skin on,
   peeled and roughly mashed
1 **egg**, beaten
150 ml (¼ pint) **milk**
50 g (2 oz) **sultanas**
oil, for greasing
butter, clear honey, golden or
   maple syrup, to serve

Put the flour, sugar and baking powder in a mixing bowl. Add the mashed banana with the egg. Gradually whisk in the milk with a fork until the mixture resembles a smooth thick batter. Stir in the sultanas.

Pour a little oil on to a piece of folded kitchen paper and use to grease a griddle or heavy nonstick frying pan. Heat the pan then drop heaped dessertspoonfuls of the mixture, well spaced apart, on to the pan. Cook for 2 minutes until bubbles appear on the top and the undersides are golden. Turn over and cook for 1–2 minutes more until the second side is done.

Serve warm, topped with butter, honey, golden or maple syrup. These are best eaten on the day they are made.

For summer berry drop scones, make the above recipe in the same way but stir in 125 g (4 oz) mixed fresh blueberries and raspberries instead of the sultanas.

spiced pear & cranberry muffins

Makes **12**
Preparation time **20 minutes**
Cooking time **15–18 minutes**

40 g (1½ oz) **dried cranberries**
2 tablespoons **boiling water**
3 small ripe **pears**
300 g (10 oz) **plain flour**
3 teaspoons **baking powder**
1 teaspoon **ground cinnamon**
½ teaspoon **grated nutmeg**
125 g (4 oz) **caster sugar**,
   plus extra for sprinkling
50 g (2 oz) **butter**, melted
3 tablespoons **olive oil**
3 **eggs**
150 g (5 oz) **low-fat natural
   yogurt**

Put the cranberries in a cup, add the boiling water and leave to soak for 10 minutes. Meanwhile, quarter, core, peel and dice the pears.

Place the flour, baking powder, spices and sugar in a mixing bowl. Fork the melted butter, oil, eggs and yogurt together in another bowl then combine with the flour mixture.

Drain the cranberries, add to the flour mixture with the pears and mix briefly then spoon into paper muffin cases arranged in a 12-hole deep muffin tin and sprinkle with a little extra caster sugar.

Bake in a preheated oven, 200°C (400°F), Gas Mark 6, for 15–18 minutes until well risen and golden. Leave to cool in the tin for 5 minutes then transfer to a wire rack. Serve warm or cold. They are best eaten on the day they are made.

For blueberry & cranberry muffins, omit the pear and spices from the recipe above and add 125 g (4 oz) fresh blueberries and the grated rind of 1 lemon instead, stirring them into the flour mixture at the same time as the soaked cranberries. Continue the recipe as above.

strawberry & lavender shortcakes

Makes **8**
Preparation time **30 minutes**
Cooking time **10–12 minutes**

150 g (5 oz) **plain flour**
25 g (1 oz) **ground rice**
125 g (4 oz) **butter**, diced
50 g (2 oz) **caster sugar**
1 tablespoon **lavender petals**

To decorate
250 g (8 oz) **strawberries** (or
   a mixture of strawberries and
   raspberries)
150 ml (¼ pint) **double cream**
16 small **lavender flowers**
   (optional)
sifted **icing sugar**, for dusting

Put the flour and ground rice in a mixing bowl or a food processor. Add the butter and rub in with your fingertips or process until the mixture resembles fine breadcrumbs.

Stir in the sugar and lavender petals and squeeze the crumbs together with your hands to form a smooth ball. Knead lightly then roll out on a lightly floured surface until 5 mm (¼ inch) thick. Stamp out 7.5 cm (3 inch) circles using a fluted round biscuit cutter. Transfer to an ungreased baking sheet. Reknead the trimmings and continue rolling and stamping out until you have made 16 biscuits.

Prick with a fork, bake in a preheated oven, 160°C (325°F), Gas Mark 3, for 10–12 minutes until pale golden. Leave to cool on the baking tray.

To serve, halve 4 of the smallest strawberries, hull and slice the rest. Whip the cream and spoon over 8 of the biscuits. Top with the sliced strawberries then the remaining biscuits. Spoon the remaining cream on top and decorate with the reserved halved strawberries and tiny sprigs of lavender, if liked. Dust lightly with sifted icing sugar. These are best eaten on the day they are filled, but the plain biscuits can be stored in an airtight tin for up to 3 days.

For lemon & blueberry shortcakes, follow the recipe above but add the grated rind of 1 lemon to the biscuit dough instead of the lavender petals. Fill with whipped cream and 150 g (5 oz) fresh blueberries.

apricot & sunflower muffins

Makes **12**
Preparation time **20 minutes**
Cooking time **15–18 minutes**

300 g (10 oz) **self-raising wholemeal flour**
1 teaspoon **baking powder**
150 g (5 oz) **light muscovado sugar**
grated rind of 1 **orange**
3 **eggs**
200 ml (7 fl oz) **full-fat crème fraîche**
225 g (7½ oz) can **apricot halves in natural juice**, drained and roughly chopped, the juice reserved
3 tablespoons **sunflower seeds**

Stir the flour, baking powder, sugar and orange rind together in a mixing bowl.

Beat the eggs in a smaller bowl then mix in the crème fraîche. Add to the flour mixture with the chopped apricots and fork together until just mixed, adding 2–3 tablespoons of the reserved canned apricot juice to make a soft spoonable consistency.

Spoon the mixture into paper muffin cases arranged in a 12-hole deep muffin tin and sprinkle with the sunflower seeds. Bake in a preheated oven, 200°C (400°F), Gas Mark 6, for 15–18 minutes until well risen and the tops are cracked. Leave to cool in the tin for 5 minutes then transfer to a wire rack. Serve warm or cold. These are best eaten on the day they are made.

For peach & orange muffins, add the diced flesh from 1 large peach, the grated rind of 1 orange and 2–3 tablespoons orange juice to the basic muffin mixture above instead of the canned apricots and their juice. Continue the recipe as above.

banoffee meringues

Makes **8**
Preparation time **30 minutes**
Cooking time **1–1¼ hours**

3 **egg whites**
100 g (3½ oz) **light muscovado sugar**
75 g (3 oz) **caster sugar**

To decorate
1 small ripe **banana**
1 tablespoon **lemon juice**
150 ml (¼ pint) **double cream**
8 tablespoons ready-made **toffee fudge ice cream sauce**

Whisk the egg whites in a large clean bowl until stiff. Gradually whisk in the sugars, a teaspoonful at a time, until it has all been added. Whisk for a few minutes more until the meringue mixture is thick and glossy.

Using a dessertspoon, take a large scoop of meringue mixture then scoop off the first spoon using a second spoon and drop on to a large baking sheet lined with nonstick baking paper to make an oval-shaped meringue. Continue until all the mixture has been used.

Bake in a preheated oven, 110°C (225°F), Gas Mark ¼, for 1–1¼ hours or until the meringues are firm and may be easily peeled off the paper. Leave to cool still on the paper.

To serve, roughly mash the banana with the lemon juice. Whip the cream until it forms soft swirls then whisk in 2 tablespoons of the toffee fudge sauce. Combine with the mashed banana then use to sandwich the meringues together in pairs and arrange in paper cake cases. Drizzle with the remaining toffee fudge sauce and serve immediately. Unfilled meringues may be stored in an airtight tin for up to 3 days.

For coffee toffee meringues, make the meringues as above. To make the filling, whip the cream, then stir in 1–2 teaspoons instant coffee, dissolved in 1 teaspoon boiling water. Use to sandwich the meringues together in pairs. Drizzle toffee fudge sauce over the top of the meringues.

hazelnut & blueberry cakes

Makes **12**
Preparation time **20 minutes**
Cooking time **20 minutes**

3 **eggs**
150 ml (¼ pint) **reduced-fat crème fraîche**
150 g (5 oz) **caster sugar**
50 g (2 oz) **finely ground hazelnuts**
175 g (6 oz) **plain flour**
1½ teaspoons **baking powder**
125 g (4 oz) **fresh blueberries**
15 g (½ oz) **hazelnuts**, roughly chopped
sifted **icing sugar**, for dusting

Put the eggs, crème fraîche and sugar in a mixing bowl and whisk together until smooth. Add the ground hazelnuts, flour and baking powder and mix together.

Spoon the mixture into paper cake cases arranged in a 12-hole deep muffin tin and divide the blueberries evenly among them, pressing lightly into the mixture. Sprinkle with chopped hazelnuts.

Bake in a preheated oven, 180°C (350°F), Gas Mark 4, for about 20 minutes until well risen and golden. Dust the tops with a little sifted icing sugar and leave to cool in the tin. These are best eaten on the day they are made.

For almond & raspberry cakes, follow the recipe above but use 50 g (2 oz) ground almonds in place of the ground hazelnuts and use the same quantity of raspberries instead of the blueberries. Sprinkle the tops of the cakes with 15 g (½ oz) flaked almonds and bake as above.

tangy lemon cupcakes

Makes **12**
Preparation time **25 minutes**
Cooking time **15–18 minutes**

125 g (4 oz) **soft margarine**
125 g (4 oz) **caster sugar**
2 **eggs**, beaten
125 g (4 oz) **self-raising flour**
grated rind and juice of
  1 **lemon**
175 g (6 oz) **icing sugar**,
  sifted
yellow or pink food colouring
sugar flowers, to decorate

Beat the margarine, sugar, eggs, flour and lemon rind in a mixing bowl or a food processor until smooth.

Divide the mixture evenly among foil cake cases arranged in a 12-hole deep muffin tin and spread the surfaces level. Bake in a preheated oven, 180°C (350°F), Gas Mark 4, for 15–18 minutes until golden and the cakes spring back when gently pressed with a fingertip. Leave to cool in the tin.

Mix the icing sugar with 4–5 teaspoons of the lemon juice to make a smooth thick spreadable paste. Trim the tops of the cakes level if needed. Spoon half the icing over half the cakes and ease into a smooth layer with a wetted round-bladed knife.

Colour the remaining icing pale yellow or pink and spoon it over the remaining cakes. Decorate with homemade pastel-coloured flowers stamped out from ready-to-roll icing or use shop-bought sugar flowers. Leave to harden for 30 minutes. Store in an airtight tin for up to 3 days.

For candy cupcakes, add 1 teaspoon vanilla essence to the cake mixture instead of the lemon rind. Add 6–7 teaspoons water instead of lemon juice to the icing sugar and mix until smooth. Colour half pale pink and half blue. Spoon over the cakes and decorate with tiny sweets instead of sugar flowers.

wholewheat treacle scones

Makes **14**
Preparation time **15 minutes**
Cooking time **6–8 minutes**

400 g (13 oz) **malted bread
flour**, plus extra for sprinkling
(optional)
50 g (2 oz) **butter**, diced
50 g (2 oz) **light muscovado
sugar**
3 teaspoons **baking powder**
1 teaspoon **bicarbonate of
soda**
8 tablespoons **low-fat natural
yogurt**
2 tablespoons **black treacle**
1 **egg**, beaten

To serve
500 ml (17 fl oz) carton
crème frâiche
375 g (13 fl oz) jar **strawberry
jam**

Put the flour in a mixing bowl or a food processor.
Add the butter and rub in with your fingertips or
process until the mixture resembles fine breadcrumbs.
Stir in the sugar and baking powder.

Stir the bicarbonate of soda into the yogurt then add
to the flour mixture with the black treacle. Gradually
mix in enough of the beaten egg to form a soft but
not sticky dough. Knead lightly then roll out on a
lightly floured surface until 2 cm (¾ inch) thick.

Working quickly, cut out 5.5 cm (2¼ inch) circles using
a plain biscuit cutter. Transfer to a greased baking
sheet. Reknead the trimmings and continue rolling and
stamping out until all the mixture has been used.
Add to the baking sheet and sprinkle the tops with
a little extra flour or leave plain if preferred.

Bake in a preheated oven, 220°C (425°F), Gas
Mark 7, for 6–8 minutes until well risen and browned.
Transfer the scones to a napkin-lined basket and
serve warm or cold, split and topped with crème
frâiche and jam. They are best eaten on the day
they are made.

For date & walnut scones, follow the basic recipe
above but stir 100 g (3½ oz) ready-chopped dried
dates and 40 g (1½ oz) chopped walnut pieces into
the scone mix just after adding the black treacle.
Continue the recipe as above.

mocha cupcakes

Makes **12**
Preparation time **15 minutes,**
  plus cooling
Cooking time **20 minutes**

250 ml (8 fl oz) **water**
250 g (8 oz) **caster sugar**
125 g (4 oz) **unsalted butter**
2 tablespoons **cocoa powder,**
  sifted
½ teaspoon **bicarbonate**
  of soda
2 tablespoons **instant coffee**
225 g (7½ oz) **self-raising**
  flour
2 **eggs**, lightly beaten
12 **chocolate-coated coffee**
  beans, to decorate

For the icing
150 g (5 oz) **plain dark**
  chocolate, broken into
  pieces
150 g (5 oz) **unsalted butter,**
  diced
2 tablespoons **golden syrup**

Put the water and sugar in a saucepan and heat gently, stirring, until the sugar has dissolved. Stir in the butter, cocoa powder, bicarbonate of soda and instant coffee and bring to the boil. Simmer for 5 minutes, remove from the heat and set aside to cool.

Beat the flour and eggs into the cooled coffee and chocolate mixture until smooth. Divide the mixture evenly among foil cake cases arranged in a 12-hole deep muffin tin. Bake in a preheated oven, 180°C (350°F), Gas Mark 4, for 20 minutes until risen and firm. Transfer to a wire rack to cool.

Make the icing. Put the chocolate, butter and syrup in a heatproof bowl set over a saucepan of gently simmering water, stirring until melted. Remove from the heat and leave to cool to room temperature, then chill until thickened. Spread over the cupcakes, top with a chocolate coffee bean and leave to set.

For double chocolate cupcakes, omit the instant coffee from the cake mix and decorate the icing with some white chocolate curls instead of the chocolate covered beans.

raspberry & coconut friands

Makes **9**
Preparation time **10 minutes**
Cooking time **18–20 minutes**

75 g (3 oz) **plain flour**
200 g (7 oz) **icing sugar**
125 g (4 oz) **ground almonds**
50 g (2 oz) **desiccated coconut**
grated rind of **1 lemon**
5 **egg whites**
175 g (6 oz) **unsalted butter**, melted
125 g (4 oz) **raspberries**

Sift the flour and icing sugar into a mixing bowl and stir in the ground almonds, coconut and lemon rind.

Whisk the egg whites in a large clean bowl until frothy then fold into the dry ingredients. Add the melted butter and stir until evenly combined.

Spoon the mixture into 9 lightly oiled friand tins (or a shallow bun tray). Top each friand with a few raspberries and bake in a preheated oven, 200°C (400°F), Gas Mark 6, for 18–20 minutes until a skewer inserted into the centre comes out clean. Leave to cool in the tins for 5 minutes then turn out on to a wire rack to cool completely.

For apricot & pistachio friands, replace the desiccated coconut with 50 g (2 oz) shelled and chopped pistachios and replace the raspberries with the same weight of diced fresh apricots. Continue the recipe as above.

cookies

fairings

Makes **12**
Preparation time **15 minutes**
Cooking time **16–20 minutes**

100 g (3½ oz) **plain flour**
1 teaspoon **baking powder**
½ teaspoon **bicarbonate of soda**
½ teaspoon **ground cinnamon**
½ teaspoon **ground ginger**
¼ teaspoon **ground allspice** or **mixed spice**
finely grated rind of 1 **lemon**
50 g (2 oz) **butter**, diced
50 g (2 oz) **caster sugar**
2 tablespoons **golden syrup**

Mix the flour, baking powder, bicarbonate of soda, spices and lemon rind together in a mixing bowl. Add the butter and rub in with your fingertips until the mixture resembles fine breadcrumbs.

Stir in the sugar, add the syrup then mix together first with a spoon then squeeze the crumbs together with your hands to form a ball.

Shape the dough into a log then slice into 12. Roll each piece into a ball and arrange on 2 large greased baking sheets, leaving space between for them to spread during cooking.

Cook one baking sheet at a time in the centre of a preheated oven, 180°C (350°F), Gas Mark 4, for 8–10 minutes or until the biscuit tops are cracked and golden.

Leave to harden for 1–2 minutes then loosen and transfer to a wire rack to cool completely. Store in an airtight tin for up to 3 days.

For chocolate ginger yo-yo's, follow the recipe above but use 1 teaspoon ground ginger instead of the 3 spices and the grated rind of ½ small orange instead of 1 lemon. Shape into 20 smaller biscuits, bake for 5–6 minutes as above, then transfer to a wire rack to cool completely. Melt 75 g (3 oz) dark chocolate, then use a little to sandwich biscuits together in pairs. Drizzle the rest over the top of the biscuits. Serve when the chocolate has hardened.

easter cookies

Makes **18**
Preparation time **20 minutes**
Cooking time **10 minutes**

250 g (8 oz) **plain flour**
50 g (2 oz) **cornflour**
175 g (6 oz) **butter**, diced
100 g (3½ oz) **caster sugar**
a few drops of **vanilla essence**

To decorate
1 **egg white**
250 g (8 oz) **icing sugar**,
   sifted
1 teaspoon **lemon juice**
selection of **liquid or paste
   food colourings**

Put the flour and cornflour in a mixing bowl or a food processor. Add the butter and rub in with your fingertips or process until the mixture resembles fine breadcrumbs. Stir in the sugar and vanilla until mixed, then squeeze the crumbs together with your hands to form a smooth ball.

Knead lightly then roll out thinly on a lightly floured surface. Stamp out festive shapes using biscuit cutters and transfer to ungreased baking sheets. Reknead the trimmings and continue rolling and stamping out until all the dough has been used.

Prick the shapes with a fork, then bake in a preheated oven, 180°C (350°F), Gas Mark 4, for 10 minutes or until pale golden. Leave to cool on the baking sheet.

Make the icing. Place the egg white in a bowl. Gradually mix in the icing sugar and lemon juice to give a smooth consistency. Add extra water if the icing seems too thick. Divide between 2 or more bowls and colour as you like.

Spoon the icing into greaseproof paper piping bags, snip off the tips and pipe outlines around the edge of the cookies. Leave to harden for 10 minutes. Fill in the rest of the surface of the cookie with the same colour icing to create a smooth evenly covered cookie top. Leave to dry. Finally, pipe white icing over the top of the coloured surface to outline and make specific features.

For numberelli cookies, follow the recipe above, then roll out the cookie dough and stamp out large numbers with specialist cutters. Bake and ice with brightly coloured icing, decorating with sugar strands.

chocolate florentines

Makes **26**
Preparation time **30 minutes**
Cooking time **15–20 minutes**

100 g (3½ oz) **butter**
100 g (3½ oz) **caster sugar**
75 g (3 oz) **multi-coloured glacé cherries**, roughly chopped
75 g (3 oz) **flaked almonds**
50 g (2 oz) **whole candied peel**, finely chopped
50 g (2 oz) **hazelnuts**, roughly chopped
2 tablespoons **plain flour**
150 g (5 oz) **plain dark chocolate**, broken into pieces

Put the butter and sugar in a saucepan and heat gently until the butter has melted and the sugar dissolved. Remove the pan from the heat and stir in all the remaining ingredients except the chocolate.

Spoon tablespoons of the mixture, well spaced apart, on to 3 baking sheets lined with nonstick baking paper. Flatten the mounds slightly. Cook one baking sheet at a time in the centre of a preheated oven, 180°C (350°F), Gas Mark 4, for 5–7 minutes until the nuts are golden.

After removing each baking sheet from the oven, neaten and shape the edges of the cooked biscuits by placing a slightly larger plain round biscuit cutter over the top and rotating to smooth and tidy up the edges. Leave to cool.

Melt the chocolate in a heatproof bowl set over a saucepan of gently simmering water. Peel the biscuits off the lining paper and arrange upside down on a wire rack. Spoon the melted chocolate over the flat underside of the biscuits and spread the surfaces level. Leave to cool and harden.

For white chocolate & ginger florentines, add 2 tablespoons ready-chopped glacé ginger to the glacé and candied fruit and nut mixture. Spread the cooked biscuits with melted white chocolate instead of plain dark chocolate as above.

ginger snowmen

Makes **12**
Preparation time **30 minutes**
Cooking time **7–8 minutes**

150 g (5 oz) **plain flour**
50 g (2 oz) **caster sugar**
1 teaspoon **ground ginger**
100 g (3½ oz) **butter**, diced
24 small **silver balls or
 tiny sweets**
50 g (2 oz) **ready-to-roll
 pink icing**
50 g (2 oz) **ready-to-roll blue
 icing**
small tube **black writing icing**

For the icing
125 g (4 oz) **icing sugar**
pinch of **ground ginger**
5 teaspoons **water**

Put the flour, sugar and ground ginger in a mixing bowl or a food processor. Add the butter and rub in with your fingertips or process until the mixture resembles fine breadcrumbs.

Continue mixing, or squeeze the crumbs together with your hands to form a soft ball. Knead lightly, then roll out thinly between 2 pieces of nonstick baking paper.

Cut out snowmen shapes using a 10 cm (4 inch) biscuit cutter then transfer to ungreased baking sheets. Bake in a preheated oven, 180°C (350°F), Gas Mark 4, for 7–8 minutes until pale golden. Leave to cool on the baking sheets then transfer to a wire rack.

Make the icing. Sift the icing sugar and ground ginger into a bowl. Gradually mix in the water to make a smooth thin icing. Spoon over the biscuits and allow to drizzle over the edges. Add the silver balls or tiny sweets for eyes, then leave to dry and harden.

Decorate the snowmen with scarves, hats and pompoms made from the ready-to-roll icing, sticking the pompoms with a little water. Pipe on small, black, smiling mouths. Leave to harden for 1 hour, before serving.

For halloween pumpkins, replace the ginger in the mix with 1 teaspoon ground cinnamon. Stamp out 7 cm (3 inch) circles using a plain round biscuit cutter and bake as above. Make up the icing using 175 g (6 oz) icing sugar and 6–7 teaspoons fresh orange juice and colour orange with a little food colouring. Spoon over the biscuits and leave until almost set. Use yellow, black and green ready-to-roll icing to decorate the faces.

coffee kisses

Makes **10**
Preparation time **25 minutes, plus chilling**
Cooking time **8–10 minutes**

2 teaspoons **instant coffee**
1 teaspoon **boiling water**
75 g (3 oz) **butter**, at room temperature
50 g (2 oz) **light muscovado sugar**
125 g (4 oz) **self-raising flour**

For the filling
2 teaspoons **instant coffee**
2 teaspoons **boiling water**
50 g (2 oz) **butter**, at room temperature
100 g (3½ oz) **icing sugar**, sifted

Dissolve the coffee in the boiling water. Beat the butter and sugar together in a mixing bowl until pale and creamy. Add the dissolved coffee then gradually mix in the flour to make a smooth soft dough.

Shape the dough into a log then chill for 15 minutes. Slice the chilled log into 20 pieces. Roll each piece into a ball, arrange on 2 greased baking sheets and flatten slightly by pressing with a fork. Bake in a preheated oven, 180°C (350°F), Gas Mark 4, for 8–10 minutes until browned. Leave the biscuits to cool for 5 minutes then transfer to a wire rack to cool completely.

Make the filling. Dissolve the coffee in the boiling water. Beat the butter and icing sugar together then stir in the dissolved coffee until smooth and fluffy. Use to sandwich the biscuits together in pairs. Eat within 2 days.

For chocolate kisses, omit the dissolved coffee from the biscuit dough and substitute 15 g (½ oz) cocoa powder for the same weight of flour. Shape as above, then use 50 g (2 oz) milk chocolate, melted, in the filling in place of the dissolved coffee.

maple biscuits

Makes **40**
Preparation time **20 minutes,
plus setting**
Cooking time **12–15 minutes**

6 tablespoons **maple syrup**
50 g (2 oz) **caster sugar**
1 teaspoon **bicarbonate of
soda**
1 **egg yolk**
100 g (3½ oz) **butter**, melted
150 g (5 oz) **plain flour**
¼ teaspoon **ground cinnamon**
75 g (3 oz) **plain dark
chocolate**, broken into
pieces
75 g (3 oz) **white chocolate**,
broken into pieces

Stir the maple syrup, sugar, bicarbonate of soda and egg yolk into the melted butter then mix in the flour and cinnamon. Beat to a smooth creamy dough.

Drop teaspoons of the mixture, spaced slightly apart, on to baking sheets lined with nonstick baking paper. Bake in a preheated oven, 190°C (375°F), Gas Mark 5, for 4–5 minutes until golden brown. Leave to harden for 1–2 minutes then loosen and transfer to a wire rack.

Melt the plain dark and the white chocolate in separate heatproof bowls set over saucepans of gently simmering water.

Hold a biscuit over one of the bowls and spoon a little of the chocolate over half of it, spreading it with the back of the spoon. Return the biscuit to the wire rack and coat all the biscuits in the same way, so half are covered with dark and the rest in white chocolate. Leave in a cool place for 30 minutes until the chocolate has hardened. Store in an airtight container, the layers separated with sheets of nonstick or greaseproof paper, for up to 2 days.

For honey biscuits, use honey instead of the maple syrup, and ground ginger in place of the ground cinnamon. Sprinkle brown sugar over the biscuits just before cooking, instead of coating them in melted chocolate afterwards.

almond shorties

Makes **14**
Preparation time **25 minutes**
Cooking time **15 minutes**

175 g (6 oz) **plain flour**
50 g (2 oz) **ground almonds**
50 g (2 oz) **caster sugar**
a few drops of **almond
essence**
150 g (5 oz) **butter**, diced

To decorate
25 g (1 oz) **whole blanched
almonds**, halved
2 **glacé cherries**, cut into
small pieces
extra **caster sugar**,
for sprinkling

Put the flour, ground almonds, sugar and almond essence in a mixing bowl or a food processor. Add the butter and rub in with your fingertips or process until the mixture resembles fine breadcrumbs.

Squeeze the mixture together with your hands to form a ball. Knead lightly then roll out on a lightly floured surface until 1 cm (½ inch) thick. Stamp out 6 cm (2½ inch) circles using a fluted round biscuit cutter. Transfer to an ungreased baking sheet. Reknead the trimmings and continue rolling and stamping out until all the mixture has been used.

Prick each shortbread biscuit 4 times with a fork to make a cross shape then add an almond half to the space between each fork mark. Decorate the centre with a small piece of glacé cherry. Sprinkle with a little extra caster sugar and bake in a preheated oven, 160°C (325°F), Gas Mark 3, for about 15 minutes until pale golden.

Loosen the biscuits and leave to cool on the baking sheet or transfer to a wire rack if preferred.

For orange flower shorties, omit the ground almonds from the shortie mixture and reduce the quantity of butter to 125 g (4 oz), adding 2 teaspoons orange flower water, or to taste. Bake as above then dust with sifted icing sugar. Serve the biscuits on their own or as an accompaniment to fruit fools or mousses.

linzer biscuits

Makes **16**
Preparation time **35 minutes**
Cooking time **16 minutes**

50 g (2 oz) **hazelnuts**
225 g (7½ oz) **plain flour**
75 g (3 oz) **caster sugar**
150 g (5 oz) **butter**, diced
finely grated rind of ½ **lemon**
1 **egg yolk**
4 tablespoons **seedless raspberry jam**
sifted **icing sugar**, for dusting

Grind the hazelnuts very finely in a blender or coffee grinder. Set aside.

Put the flour and sugar in a mixing bowl or a food processor. Add the butter and rub in with your fingertips or process until the mixture resembles fine breadcrumbs. Stir in the ground hazelnuts and lemon rind, then mix in the egg yolk and bring the mixture together with your hands to form a firm dough.

Knead lightly then roll out half of the dough on a lightly floured surface until 1 cm (½ inch) thick. Stamp out 5.5 cm (2¼ inch) circles using a fluted round biscuit cutter. Transfer to an ungreased baking sheet. Use a small heart- or star-shaped biscuit cutter to remove 2.5 cm (1 inch) hearts or stars from the middle of half of the biscuits.

Bake the first biscuits in a preheated oven, 160°C (350°F), Gas Mark 3, for about 8 minutes, until pale golden brown, then repeat for the remaining dough.

Leave the biscuits to harden for 1–2 minutes then loosen and transfer to a wire rack to cool.

Divide the jam evenly among the centres of the whole biscuits and spread thickly, leaving a border of biscuit showing. Cover with the hole-cut biscuits, dust with a little sifted icing sugar and leave to cool completely before serving.

For orange & apricot sandwich biscuits, add the grated rind of ½ small orange, instead of the lemon, and sandwich the biscuits together with apricot jam as above.

christmas tree decorations

Makes **20**
Preparation time **35 minutes,**
  plus chilling
Cooking time **10–12 minutes**

125 g (4 oz) **butter**, at room
  temperature
125 g (4 oz) **caster sugar**
2 **egg yolks**
1 tablespoon **cocoa powder**
1 teaspoon **ground cinnamon**
175 g (6 oz) **plain flour**

For the icing
150 g (5 oz) **icing sugar,**
  sifted
4–5 teaspoons **egg white**
  or **water**

Beat the butter and sugar together in a mixing bowl until pale and creamy. Stir in the egg yolks, cocoa powder and cinnamon then gradually mix in the flour to form a smooth soft dough. Chill for 15 minutes.

Roll out the dough between 2 sheets of nonstick baking paper until 5 mm (¼ inch) thick. Stamp out festive shapes using biscuit cutters about 7.5 cm (3 inches) in diameter. Transfer to greased baking sheets. Reknead the trimmings and continue rolling and stamping out until all the mixture has been used.

Make a small hole in each biscuit using the handle of a teaspoon then bake at 180°C (350°F), Gas Mark 4, for 10–12 minutes until lightly browned. Remake the hole in each biscuit then leave to cool on the baking sheets.

Mix the icing sugar and the egg white or water to a smooth thick icing. Spoon into a greaseproof paper piping bag, snip off the tip and pipe lines, dots and swirls to decorate the biscuits. Leave to harden then thread narrow ribbons through the holes and hang on the Christmas tree or on white painted twigs standing in a jug.

For orange & mixed spice hearts, follow the recipe above but omit the cocoa powder, add an extra tablespoon of flour and stir in the grated rind of 1 small orange. Replace the ground cinnamon with 1 teaspoon ground mixed spice. Cut out heart-shaped biscuits from the dough, make ribbon holes in them, bake and decorate as above.

classic shortbread

Makes **16**
Preparation time **15 minutes,**
  plus chilling
Cooking time **18–20 minutes**

250 g (8 oz) **unsalted butter,**
  at room temperature
125 g (4 oz) **caster sugar,**
  plus extra for sprinkling
250 g (8 oz) **plain flour**
125 g (4 oz) **rice flour**
pinch of **salt**

Beat the butter and sugar together in a mixing bowl or a food processor until pale and creamy. Sift in the flour, rice flour and salt and mix or process briefly until the ingredients just come together.

Transfer to a work surface and knead lightly to form a soft dough. Shape into a disc, wrap in clingfilm and chill for 30 minutes.

Divide the dough in half and roll out each piece on a lightly floured surface to a 20 cm (8 inch) round. Transfer to 2 ungreased baking sheets. Score each round with a sharp knife, marking it into 8 equal wedges, prick with a fork and use your fingers to flute the edges.

Sprinkle over a little caster sugar and bake in a preheated oven, 190°C (375°F), Gas Mark 5, for 18–20 minutes until golden. Remove from the oven and, while still hot, cut into wedges through the score marks. Leave to cool on the baking sheet for 5 minutes then transfer to a wire rack to cool. Store in an airtight tin.

For pistachio shortbread, simply replace 50 g (2 oz) of the rice flour with 50 g (2 oz) shelled and very finely chopped pistachio nuts. Continue the recipe as above.

chunky cherry fudge cookies

Makes **18**
Preparation time **15 minutes**
Cooking time **10–12 minutes**

75 g (3 oz) **butter**, at room
  temperature
75 g (3 oz) **caster sugar**
75 g (3 oz) **light muscovado
  sugar**
1 teaspoon **vanilla essence**
1 **egg**, beaten
175 g (6 oz) **self-raising flour**
100 g (3½ oz) or 4 **chocolate-
  covered fudge bars**,
  chopped
75 g (3 oz) **glacé cherries**,
  roughly chopped

Put the butter, sugars and vanilla in a mixing bowl and beat together until pale and creamy. Stir in the egg and flour and mix until smooth.

Stir in the fudge and cherries then spoon 18 mounds on to 2 baking sheets lined with nonstick baking paper, leaving space between for them to spread during cooking.

Bake in a preheated oven, 180°C (350°F), Gas Mark 4, for 10–12 minutes until golden brown. Leave to harden for 1–2 minutes then loosen and transfer to a wire rack to cool completely. These are best eaten on the day they are made.

For dark chocolate & pistachio cookies, add 125 g (4 oz) diced, dark chocolate and 50 g (2 oz) roughly chopped, shelled pistachio nuts instead of the fudge and cherries. Bake as above, then sandwich together in pairs with scoops of vanilla ice cream. Serve immediately.

triple chocolate pretzels

Makes **40**
Preparation time **30 minutes,
plus rising and setting**
Cooking time **6–8 minutes**

225 g (7½ oz) **strong white
bread flour**
1 teaspoon **fast-action dried
yeast**
2 teaspoons **caster sugar**
large pinch of **salt**
15 g (½ oz) melted **butter or
sunflower oil**
125 ml (4 fl oz) **warm water**
75 g (3 oz) each **plain dark,
white and milk chocolate**,
broken into pieces

For the glaze
2 tablespoons **water**
½ teaspoon **salt**

Mix the flour, yeast, sugar and salt in a mixing bowl. Add the melted butter or oil and gradually mix in the warm water until you have a smooth dough. Knead the dough for 5 minutes on a lightly floured surface until smooth and elastic.

Cut the dough into quarters, then cut each quarter into 10 smaller pieces. Shape each piece into a thin rope about 20 cm (8 inches) long. Bend the rope so that it forms a wide arc, then bring one of the ends round in a loop and secure about halfway along the rope. Do the same with the other end, looping it across the first secured end.

Transfer the pretzels to 2 large greased baking sheets. Cover loosely with lightly oiled clingfilm and leave in a warm place for 30 minutes until well risen.

Make the glaze. Mix the water and salt in a bowl until the salt has dissolved then brush this over the pretzels. Bake in a preheated oven, 200°C (400°F), Gas Mark 6, for 6–8 minutes until golden brown. Transfer to a wire rack to cool.

Melt the different chocolates in 3 separate heatproof bowls set over saucepans of gently simmering water. Drizzle random lines of dark chocolate over the pretzels, using a spoon. Leave to harden then repeat with the white and then the milk chocolate.

For classic pretzels, brush plain pretzels as soon as they come out of the oven with a glaze made by heating 2 teaspoons salt, ½ teaspoon caster sugar and 2 tablespoons water in a saucepan until dissolved.

triple chocolate cookies

Makes **20**
Preparation time **15 minutes**
Cooking time **8–10 minutes**

75 g (3 oz) **butter**, at room
  temperature
175 g (6 oz) **light
  muscovado sugar**
1 **egg**
150 g (5 oz) **self-raising flour**
2 tablespoons **cocoa powder**
100 g (3½ oz) **white
  chocolate**, chopped
100 g (3½ oz) **milk chocolate**,
  chopped

Beat the butter and sugar together in a mixing bowl until pale and creamy. Stir in the egg, flour and cocoa powder and mix until smooth.

Stir in the chopped chocolate then spoon 20 mounds of the mixture on to 2 greased baking sheets, leaving space between for them to spread during cooking.

Bake in a preheated oven, 180°C (350°F), Gas Mark 4, for 8–10 minutes until lightly browned. Leave to harden for 1–2 minutes then loosen and transfer to a wire rack to cool completely. These are best eaten on the day they are made.

For chocolate, vanilla & hazelnut cookies, follow the basic recipe above but omit the cocoa powder and increase the quantity of self-raising flour to 175 g (6 oz). Omit the white chocolate and add 50 g (2 oz) roughly chopped hazelnuts and 1 teaspoon vanilla essence in its place.

shortcakes with elderflower cream

Makes **8**
Preparation time **20 minutes**
Cooking time **10–15 minutes**

250 g (8 oz) **self-raising flour**
2 teaspoons **baking powder**
75 g (3 oz) **unsalted butter**, diced
40 g (1½ oz) **caster sugar**
1 **egg**, lightly beaten
2–3 tablespoons **milk**
15 g (½ oz) **butter**, melted
250 g (8 oz) **strawberries**, hulled and sliced
icing sugar, for dusting

For the elderflower cream
300 ml (½ pint) **double cream**
2 tablespoons **elderflower syrup or undiluted cordial**

Sift the flour and baking powder into a mixing bowl or a food processor. Add the butter and rub in with your fingertips or process until the mixture resembles fine breadcrumbs. Stir in the sugar. Gradually add the egg and milk and continue mixing until the mixture just comes together to form a dough.

Roll out the dough on a lightly floured surface until 1 cm (½ inch) thick. Stamp out 8 x 7 cm (3 inch) circles using a plain round biscuit cutter. Transfer to a large, lightly oiled baking sheet and brush each round with a little melted butter.

Bake in a preheated oven, 200°C (400°F), Gas Mark 6, for 10–15 minutes until risen and golden. Remove from the oven and transfer to a wire rack to cool. While they are still warm, carefully slice each cake in half horizontally and return to the wire rack to cool completely.

Make the elderflower cream. Put the cream and elderflower syrup in a mixing bowl and whip until thickened. Spread the cream over the base of each cake, top with sliced strawberries and the cake lids. Serve dusted with icing sugar.

For raspberry & cream shortcakes, make the shortcakes as above. Fill them with the same amount of double cream, flavoured with 2 tablespoons of icing sugar. Top the cream with 250 g (8 oz) raspberries and put the cake lids on the top.

chocolate & chilli cookies

Makes **12**
Preparation time **20 minutes**
Cooking time **16–20 minutes**

100 g (3½ oz) **plain flour**
1 tablespoon **cocoa powder**
1 teaspoon **baking powder**
½ teaspoon **bicarbonate**
   of soda
½ teaspoon **ground cinnamon**
50 g (2 oz) **light muscovado**
   sugar
50 g (2 oz) **butter**, diced
¼ teaspoon **'lazy'**
   ready-chopped chilli from a
   jar or **mild fresh chopped**
   red chilli
2 tablespoons **golden syrup**
100 g (3½ oz) **plain dark**
   chocolate, finely chopped

Stir all the dry ingredients together in a bowl or a food processor. Add the butter and chilli and rub in with your fingertips or process until the mixture resembles fine breadcrumbs.

Add the syrup then mix together first with a spoon then squeeze the crumbs together with your hands to form a ball.

Knead in the chopped chocolate then shape the dough into a log and slice into 12. Roll each piece into a ball and arrange on 2 large greased baking sheets. Cook one baking sheet at a time in the centre of a preheated oven, 180°C (350°F), Gas Mark 4, for 8–10 minutes until browned and the tops are craggy.

Leave to cool for 1–2 minutes then loosen and transfer to a wire rack. These cookies are best eaten on the day they are made and delicious served while still warm.

For chocolate & ginger cookies, make the cookies in the same way as above but use 2 tablespoons ready-chopped glacé ginger instead of the chilli and ground cinnamon.

peanut butter cookies

Makes **32**
Preparation time **10 minutes**
Cooking time **12 minutes**

125 g (4 oz) **unsalted butter,**
  at room temperature
150 g (5 oz) **soft brown sugar**
125 g (4 oz) **chunky peanut**
  butter
1 **egg,** lightly beaten
150 g (5 oz) **plain flour**
½ teaspoon **baking powder**
125 g (4 oz) **unsalted**
  peanuts

Beat the butter and sugar together in a mixing bowl or a food processor until pale and creamy. Add the peanut butter, egg, flour and baking powder and stir together until combined. Stir in the peanuts.

Drop large teaspoonfuls of the mixture on to 3 large, lightly oiled baking sheets, leaving 5 cm (2 inch) gaps between each for them to spread during cooking.

Flatten the mounds slightly and bake in a preheated oven, 190°C (375°F), Gas Mark 5, for 12 minutes until golden around the edges. Leave to cool on the baking sheets for 2 minutes then transfer to a wire rack to cool completely.

For peanut butter & chocolate chip cookies, use only 50 g (2 oz) unsalted peanuts and add 50 g (2 oz) milk chocolate chips. Then make and bake the cookies as above.

sultana & caraway biscuits

Makes **14**
Preparation time **20 minutes**
Cooking time **8–10 minutes**

200 g (7 oz) **plain flour**
1 teaspoon **baking powder**
1 teaspoon **caraway seeds**,
 roughly crushed
grated rind of ½ **lemon**
75 g (3 oz) **caster sugar**, plus
 extra for sprinkling
75 g (3 oz) **butter**, diced
50 g (2 oz) **sultanas**
1 **egg**, beaten
1–2 tablespoons **semi-skimmed milk**

Mix the flour and baking powder together in a mixing bowl or a food processor then add the crushed seeds, lemon rind and sugar. Add the butter and rub in with your fingertips or process until the mixture resembles fine breadcrumbs.

Stir in the sultanas then the egg and enough milk to mix to a soft but not sticky dough.

Knead lightly then roll out on a lightly floured surface until 5 mm (¼ inch) thick. Stamp out 7.5 cm (3 inch) circles using a fluted round biscuit cutter. Transfer to a greased baking sheet. Reknead the trimmings and continue rolling and stamping out until all the dough has been used.

Prick the biscuits with a fork then sprinkle with a little extra caster sugar and bake in a preheated oven, 180°C (350°F), Gas Mark 4, for 8–10 minutes until pale golden. Transfer to a wire rack to cool. Store in an airtight tin for up to 5 days.

For fennel & orange biscuits, replace the caraway seeds and lemon rind in the recipe above with 1 teaspoon roughly crushed fennel seeds and the grated rind of ½ small orange. Continue the recipe as above.

oat & ginger crunchies

Makes **25**
Preparation time **20 minutes**
Cooking time **24–30 minutes**

100 g (3½ oz) **butter**
1 tablespoon **golden syrup**
100 g (3½ oz) **caster sugar**
1 teaspoon **bicarbonate of soda**
1 teaspoon **ground ginger**
2 tablespoons **ready-chopped glacé ginger**
100 g (3½ oz) **plain wholemeal flour**
125 g (4 oz) **porridge oats**

Put the butter, syrup and sugar in a saucepan and heat gently, stirring until the butter has melted and the sugar dissolved. Remove the pan from the heat then stir in the bicarbonate of soda, ground and chopped ginger. Add the flour and oats and mix well.

Spoon heaped teaspoons of the mixture on to 3 lightly greased baking sheets, leaving a little space between for the biscuits to spread during cooking.

Cook one baking sheet at a time in the centre of a preheated oven, 180°C (350°F), Gas Mark 4, for 8–10 minutes until the biscuits are craggy and golden. Leave to harden for 1–2 minutes then loosen and transfer to a wire rack to cool. Store in an airtight tin for up to 3 days.

For orange crunchies, omit the ground and glacé ginger and use the grated rind of ½ small orange in their place. Continue the recipe as above.

grilled biscotti

Makes **about 30**
Preparation time **20 minutes**
Cooking time **43–48 minutes,**
    plus cooling

2 **eggs**
100 g (3½ oz) **caster sugar**
200 g (7 oz) **plain flour**
75 g (3 oz) **ground almonds
    or hazelnuts**
1 heaped teaspoon **baking
    powder**
grated rind of 2 **limes**
pinch of **salt**
40 g (1½ oz) **shelled
    pistachio nuts**, roughly
    chopped
25 g (1 oz) **hazelnuts,**
    chopped

Whisk the eggs and sugar together in a mixing bowl until pale and frothy. Using a wooden spoon, slowly work in the flour, ground almonds or hazelnuts, baking powder, lime rind and salt.

Add the chopped pistachios and hazelnuts and knead lightly to form a soft dough. Shape the dough into a thick log, about 25 cm (10 inches) long and 10 cm (4 inches) wide, then flatten it slightly with the palm of your hand.

Transfer the dough to a greased baking sheet and bake in a preheated oven, 180°C (350°F), Gas Mark 4, for 35–40 minutes until light golden. Remove from the oven and leave to cool for 5 minutes, then cut into 5 mm (¼ inch) thick slices using a serrated knife.

Arrange the biscotti directly on a grill pan and cook under a preheated low grill for about 4 minutes on each side until crisp and golden. Transfer to a wire rack to cool.

For lemon & macadamia biscotti, add the grated rind of 1 lemon in place of the lime rind and 65 g (2½ oz) macadamia nuts in place of the pistachio and hazelnuts. Continue the recipe as above.

coconut & pistachio fridge cookies

Makes **20**
Preparation time **25 minutes,**
  plus chilling
Cooking time **8–10 minutes**

150 g (5 oz) **butter,**
  at room temperature
150 g (5 oz) **caster sugar**
grated rind of 1 **lime**
1 **egg**
50 g (2 oz) **desiccated**
  coconut
200 g (7 oz) **plain flour**
50 g (2 oz) **shelled pistachio**
  nuts, finely chopped

Beat the butter and sugar together in a mixing bowl. Add the lime rind, egg and coconut and beat until smooth. Gradually beat in the flour.

Spoon the mixture on to a piece of greaseproof paper and shape into a log about 35 cm (14 inches) long. Roll the dough in the chopped pistachios then wrap in the paper and twist the ends together. Chill in the refrigerator for at least 15 minutes or up to 3 days.

To serve, unwrap and slice off as many biscuits as required. Arrange on a greased baking sheet and bake in a preheated oven, 180°C (350°F), Gas Mark 4, for 8–10 minutes until pale golden. Leave to cool for 5 minutes then transfer to a wire rack to cool completely. These are best eaten on the day they are made.

For vanilla & demerara cookies, omit the lime and desiccated coconut, and flavour the mixture with 1 teaspoon vanilla essence instead. Roll the dough in 4 tablespoons demerara sugar instead of the pistachios. Slice and bake as above.

traybakes

chocolate chip shortbread

Cuts into **12**
Preparation time **15 minutes**
Cooking time **20–25 minutes**

150 g (5 oz) **plain flour**
25 g (1 oz) **cornflour**
125 g (4 oz) **butter**, diced
50 g (2 oz) **caster sugar**
75 g (3 oz) **milk chocolate**,
   chopped

To finish
a little **ground cinnamon**
1 tablespoon **caster sugar**

Put the flours in a mixing bowl or a food processor. Add the butter and rub in with your fingertips or process until the mixture resembles fine breadcrumbs. Stir in the sugar and chocolate then squeeze the crumbs together with your hands to form a ball.

Press into an ungreased 18 cm (7 inch) shallow square cake tin and prick the top with a fork. Mix the cinnamon and sugar together and sprinkle half over the top. Bake in a preheated oven, 160°C (325°F), Gas Mark 3, for 20–25 minutes until pale golden.

Remove from the oven and mark into 12 bars. Sprinkle with the remaining cinnamon sugar mix and leave to cool in the tin. Cut the shortbread right through and lift out of the tin. Store in an airtight tin for up to 5 days.

For lemon shortbread fingers, add the grated rind of 1 lemon to the flour and omit the milk chocolate and ground cinnamon. Press the shortbread mixture into the shallow square cake tin and bake as above.

jim jams

Cuts into **9**
Preparation time **10 minutes**
Cooking time **15–20 minutes**

125 g (4 oz) **butter**
125 g (4 oz) **golden syrup**
125 g (4 oz) **light muscovado sugar**
125 g (4 oz) **oats**
125 g (4 oz) **self-raising wholemeal flour**
25 g (1 oz) **desiccated coconut**

To finish
3 tablespoons **strawberry jam**
2 tablespoons **desiccated coconut**

Put the butter, syrup and sugar in a saucepan and heat gently until just melted.

Remove the pan from the heat and stir in the oats, flour and coconut. Tip the mixture into an 18 cm (7 inch) shallow square cake tin lined with nonstick baking paper (see page 11), and press into an even layer.

Bake in a preheated oven, 180°C (350°F), Gas Mark 4, for 15–20 minutes until golden. Leave to cool for 10 minutes then mark into 9 squares. Spread with the jam and sprinkle with the coconut. Leave to cool completely.

Lift the paper out of the tin, cut the squares right through and peel off the paper. Store in an airtight tin for up to 3 days.

For marmalade flapjacks, stir 2 tablespoons chunky marmalade into the flapjack mixture before spooning it into the prepared cake tin and baking as above. To finish, glaze with a little extra marmalade when the flapjack comes out of the oven and omit the desiccated coconut. Cut into squares.

power bars

Cuts into **16**
Preparation **15 minutes**
Cooking time **25–30 minutes**

200 g (7 oz) **butter**
150 g (5 oz) **light muscovado sugar**
4 tablespoons **golden syrup**
100 g (3½ oz) **mixed seeds** (such as sesame, sunflower, pumpkin, hemp and light or dark linseeds)
50 g (2 oz) **whole unblanched almonds**
50 g (2 oz) **hazelnuts**
1 **dessert apple**, cored, diced but not peeled
1 small **banana**, peeled and roughly mashed
200 g (7 oz) **porridge oats**

Put the butter, sugar and syrup in a saucepan and heat gently until just melted. Remove the pan from the heat and stir in all the remaining ingredients. Tip the mixture into an 18 x 28 cm (7 x 11 inch) roasting tin lined with nonstick baking paper (see page 11), and press into an even layer.

Bake in a preheated oven, 180°C (350°F), Gas Mark 4, for 25–30 minutes until golden brown and just beginning to darken around the edges. Leave to cool for 10 minutes then mark into 16 bars and leave to cool completely.

Lift the paper out of the tin, cut the bars right through and peel off the paper. Store in an airtight tin for up to 3 days – they are energy boosters and therefore ideal for adding to lunchboxes.

For sesame & banana flapjacks, melt the butter, sugar and syrup as above, then stir in 50 g (2 oz) sesame seeds instead of the mixed seeds. Omit the nuts and apple and mix in 2 small peeled and mashed bananas and 250 g (8 oz) porridge oats. Spoon into a 20 cm (8 inch) shallow cake tin with base and sides lined with non-stick baking paper snipped into the corners. Bake for 25 minutes until golden. Cool, then cut into 16 small squares.

cherry & almond polenta cake

Cuts into **14**
Preparation time **25 minutes**
Cooking time **25–30 minutes**

175 g (6 oz) **butter**, at room
   temperature
175 g (6 oz) **caster sugar**
3 **eggs**, beaten
75 g (3 oz) **'1 minute cook'**
   polenta
125 g (4 oz) **ground almonds**
1 teaspoon **baking powder**
grated rind and juice of
   ½ **lemon**
425 g (14 oz) can **stoned**
   black cherries, drained
15 g (½ oz) **flaked almonds**
sifted **icing sugar**, to decorate

Beat the butter and sugar together in a mixing bowl until pale and creamy. Gradually mix in alternate spoonfuls of beaten egg and polenta. Stir in the ground almonds and baking powder then mix in the lemon rind and juice.

Spoon the mixture into a greased 18 x 28 cm (7 x 11 inch) roasting tin. Sprinkle the canned cherries over the top then the flaked almonds.

Bake in a preheated oven, 180°C (350°F), Gas Mark 4, for 25–30 minutes until well risen, the cake is golden and springs back when gently pressed with a fingertip.

Leave to cool in the tin, dust with sifted icing sugar then cut into 14 bars and lift out of the tin. Store in an airtight tin for up to 2 days.

For plum & hazelnut polenta cake, replace the ground almonds with the same weight of toasted and very finely chopped hazelnuts and top with 400 g (13 oz) red plums, stoned and sliced, instead of the canned cherries. Sprinkle some untoasted hazelnuts over the top instead of flaked almonds and bake as above.

rum & raisin chocolate brownies

Cuts into **20**
Preparation time **30 minutes, plus soaking**
Cooking time **25–30 minutes**

3 tablespoons **white or dark rum**
100 g (3½ oz) **raisins**
250 g (8 oz) **plain dark chocolate**, broken into pieces
250 g (8 oz) **butter**
4 **eggs**
200 g (7 oz) **caster sugar**
75 g (3 oz) **self-raising flour**
1 teaspoon **baking powder**
100 g (3½ oz) **white or milk chocolate**

Warm the rum, add the raisins and leave to soak for 2 hours or overnight.

Heat the dark chocolate and butter gently in a saucepan until both have melted. Meanwhile, whisk the eggs and sugar together in a bowl, using an electric whisk, until very thick and the whisk leaves a trail when lifted above the mixture.

Fold the warm chocolate and butter into the whisked eggs and sugar. Sift the flour and baking powder over the top then fold in. Pour the mixture into an 18 x 28 cm (7 x 11 inch) roasting tin lined with nonstick baking paper, and ease into the corners. Spoon the rum-soaked raisins over the top.

Bake in a preheated oven, 180°C (350°F), Gas Mark 4, for 25–30 minutes until well risen, the top is crusty and cracked and the centre still slightly soft. Leave to cool and harden in the tin.

Lift out of the tin using the lining paper. Melt the milk chocolate in a heatproof bowl set over a saucepan of gently simmering water then drizzle over the top of the brownies. Leave to harden then cut into 20 pieces. Peel off the paper and store in an airtight tin for up to 3 days.

For triple chocolate brownies, omit the rum-soaked raisins and instead sprinkle 100 g (3½ oz) finely chopped milk chocolate and 100 g (3½ oz) finely chopped white chocolate over the mixture just before baking. Bake as above then omit the melted chocolate topping.

white chocolate & apricot blondies

Cuts into **20**
Preparation time **25 minutes**
Cooking time **25–30 minutes**

300 g (10 oz) **white chocolate**
125 g (4 oz) **butter**
3 **eggs**
175 g (6 oz) **caster sugar**
1 teaspoon **vanilla essence**
175 g (6 oz) **self-raising flour**
1 teaspoon **baking powder**
125 g (4 oz) **ready-to-eat dried apricots**, chopped

Break half the chocolate into pieces, place in a saucepan with the butter and heat gently until melted. Dice the remaining chocolate.

Whisk the eggs, sugar and vanilla together in a bowl, using an electric whisk, for about 5 minutes until very thick and foamy and the whisk leaves a trail when lifted above the mixture. Fold in the melted chocolate mixture and then the flour and baking powder. Gently fold in half the chopped chocolate and apricots.

Pour the mixture into an 18 x 28 cm (7 x 11 inch) roasting tin lined with nonstick baking paper, and ease into the corners. Sprinkle with the remaining chocolate and apricots. Bake in a preheated oven, 180°C (350°F), Gas Mark 4, for 25–30 minutes until well risen, the top is crusty and the centre still slightly soft.

Leave to cool in the tin then lift out using the lining paper and cut into 20 small pieces. Peel off the paper and store in an airtight tin for up to 3 days.

For white chocolate & cranberry blondies, follow the recipe above, simply replacing the ready-to-eat dried apricots with 75 g (3 oz) dried cranberries.

tropical gingercake

Cuts into **20**
Preparation time **30 minutes**
Cooking time **25 minutes**

150 g (5 oz) **butter**
125 g (4 oz) **light muscovado sugar**
3 tablespoons **golden syrup**
250 g (8 oz) **self-raising flour**
1 teaspoon **baking powder**
3 teaspoons **ground ginger**
50 g (2 oz) **desiccated coconut**
3 **eggs**, beaten
200 g (7 oz) can **pineapple rings**, drained and chopped

For the lime frosting
100 g (3½ oz) **butter**,
    at room temperature
200 g (7 oz) sifted **icing sugar**
grated rind and juice of **1 lime**
ready-to-eat dried papaya and apricot, diced
few **dried coconut** shavings,
    for sprinkling

Heat the butter, sugar and syrup gently in a saucepan, stirring until melted.

Mix the dry ingredients together in a mixing bowl then stir in the melted butter mixture and beat together until smooth. Stir in the eggs then the chopped pineapple, reserving a few pieces for decoration if liked.

Pour the mixture into an 18 x 28 cm (7 x 11 inch) roasting tin, greased and base-lined with oiled greaseproof paper, and spread the surface level.

Bake in a preheated oven, 180°C (350°F), Gas Mark 4, for about 20 minutes until well risen and the cake springs back when gently pressed with a fingertip. Leave to cool in the tin for 10 minutes then loosen the edges, turn out on to a wire rack and peel off the lining paper.

Make the lime frosting. Beat the butter, icing sugar, half the lime rind and juice together to a smooth fluffy mixture. Turn the cake over so the top is uppermost then spread with the lime frosting. Decorate with a sprinkling of the remaining lime rind, the ready-to-eat dried fruits and coconut shavings. Store in an airtight tin for up to 2 days. Cut into 20 pieces to serve.

For carrot & sultana cake, follow the above recipe but omit the ground ginger. Add 150 g (5 oz) peeled and grated carrots and 75 g (3 oz) sultanas in place of the pineapple and the desiccated coconut. Use the grated rind and juice of ½ small orange in the frosting instead of the lime.

chocolate pear & orange squares

Cuts into **8**
Preparation time **25 minutes**
Cooking time **30–35 minutes**

175 g (6 oz) **butter**, at room
   temperature
175 g (6 oz) **caster sugar**
3 **eggs**, beaten
125 g (4 oz) **self-raising flour**
75 g (3 oz) **self-raising
   wholemeal flour**
25 g (1 oz) **cocoa**
grated rind and 2 tablespoons
   juice from 1 **orange**
4 small conference **pears**,
   peeled, halved and cored

To finish
sifted **icing sugar**, for dusting
a little grated **chocolate**
a little grated **orange rind**

Beat the butter and sugar together in a mixing bowl until light and fluffy. Gradually mix in alternate spoonfuls of beaten egg and flour until all has been added and the mixture is smooth. Stir in the cocoa, orange rind and juice then spoon the mixture into an 18 x 28 cm (7 x 11 inch) roasting tin lined with nonstick baking paper (see page 11), and spread the surface level.

Cut each pear half into long thin slices and fan out slightly but keep together in their original shape. Carefully lift on to the top of the cake and arrange in 2 rows of 4.

Bake in a preheated oven, 180°C (350°F), Gas Mark 4, for 30–35 minutes until well risen and the cake springs back when gently pressed with a fingertip.

Lift out of the tin using the lining paper, cut into 8 pieces and peel off the paper. Dust with sifted icing sugar and sprinkle with a little extra grated chocolate and orange rind. Serve warm or cold as it is, or serve it warm as a dessert with ice cream or custard. Store in an airtight tin for up to 2 days.

For honeyed pear squares, replace the caster sugar with 150 g (5 oz) thick set honey. Omit the cocoa and add 125 g (4 oz) self-raising wholemeal flour. Drizzle the pears in the baked cake with a little honey and then dust with sifted icing sugar.

apple & blackberry crumble cake

Cuts into **16**
Preparation time **30 minutes**
Cooking time **45 minutes**

175 g (6 oz) **butter**, at room
    temperature
175 g (6 oz) **caster sugar**
3 **eggs**, beaten
200 g (7 oz) **self-raising flour**
1 teaspoon **baking powder**
grated rind of 1 **lemon**
500 g (1 lb) **cooking apples**,
    cored, peeled and thinly
    sliced
150 g (5 oz) **frozen**
    blackberries, just defrosted

For the crumble topping
75 g (3 oz) **self-raising flour**
75 g (3 oz) **muesli**
50 g (2 oz) **caster sugar**
75 g (3 oz) **butter**, diced

Cream the butter and sugar together in a mixing bowl until pale and creamy. Gradually mix in alternate spoonfuls of beaten egg and flour until all has been added and the mixture is smooth. Stir in the baking powder and lemon rind then spoon the mixture into an 18 x 28 cm (7 x 11 inch) roasting tin lined with nonstick baking paper (see page 11). Spread the surface level than arrange the apple slices and blackberries over the top.

Make the crumble topping. Put the flour, muesli and caster sugar in a mixing bowl, add the butter and rub in with your fingertips until the mixture resembles fine breadcrumbs. Sprinkle over the top of the fruit. Bake in a preheated oven, 180°C (350°F), Gas Mark 4, for about 45 minutes until the crumble is golden brown and a skewer inserted into the centre comes out clean.

Leave to cool in the tin then lift out using the lining paper. Cut the cake into 16 bars and peel off the lining paper. Store in an airtight tin for up to 2 days.

For apple & mincemeat crumble cake, replace the frozen blackberries with the same weight of mincemeat. Sprinkle with crumble topping then add 25 g (1 oz) flaked almonds. Bake as above.

frosted banana bars

Cuts into **16**
Preparation time **30 minutes**
Cooking time **25–30 minutes**

175 g (6 oz) **butter**, at room
   temperature
175 g (6 oz) **caster sugar**
3 **eggs**, beaten
250 g (8 oz) **self-raising flour**
1 teaspoon **baking powder**
2 **bananas**, about 175 g
   (6 oz) each with skins on,
   peeled and roughly mashed

For the frosting
50 g (2 oz) **butter**
25 g (1 oz) **cocoa powder**
250 g (8 oz) **icing sugar**,
   sifted
1–2 tablespoons **milk**
sugar shapes and sprinkles,
   to decorate

Cream the butter and sugar together in a mixing bowl until pale and creamy. Gradually mix in alternate spoonfuls of beaten egg and flour until all has been added and the mixture is smooth. Add the baking powder and mashed bananas and mix well.

Spoon the mixture into an 18 x 28 cm (7 x 11 inch) roasting tin lined with nonstick baking paper, and spread the surface level. Bake in a preheated oven, 180°C (350°F), Gas Mark 4, for 25–30 minutes until well risen, the cake is golden and springs back when gently pressed with a fingertip. Leave to cool in the tin.

Make the frosting. Heat the butter in a small saucepan. Stir in the cocoa powder and cook gently for 1 minute then remove the pan from the heat and mix in the icing sugar. Return to the heat and heat gently, stirring until melted and smooth, adding enough milk to mix to a smooth spreadable icing.

Pour the icing over the top of the cake and spread the surface level with a palette knife. Sprinkle with sugar shapes and sprinkles and leave to cool and harden. Lift the cake out of the tin using the lining paper. Cut into 16 bars and peel off the paper. Store in an airtight tin for up to 3 days.

For cranberry & banana bites, stir 50 g (2 oz) dried cranberries into the cake mix along with the mashed bananas. Spoon into the tin as above and sprinkle with 4 tablespoons sunflower seeds. Bake, then dust with a little sifted icing sugar when cool. Cut into 24 squares.

mango & kiwi upside down cakes

Cuts into **20**
Preparation time **30 minutes**
Cooking time **30–35 minutes**

1 large **mango**
4 tablespoons **apricot jam**
grated rind and juice of 2
  limes
2 **kiwi fruit**, sliced
250 g (8 oz) **soft margarine**
125 g (4 oz) **caster sugar**
125 g (4 oz) **light muscovado**
  sugar
250 g (8 oz) **self-raising flour**
4 **eggs**

Cut a thick slice off each side of the mango to reveal the large flat central stone. Cut the flesh away from the stone then peel and slice.

Mix the apricot jam with the juice of 1 of the limes then spoon into the base of an 18 x 28 cm (7 x 11 inch) roasting tin lined with nonstick baking paper (see page 11). Arrange the mango and kiwi fruit randomly over the top.

Put the lime rind and rest of the juice in a mixing bowl or a food processor, add the remaining ingredients and beat until smooth. Spoon over the top of the fruit and spread the surface level. Bake in a preheated oven, 180°C (350°F), Gas Mark 4, for 30–35 minutes until well risen, the cake is golden and springs back when gently pressed with a fingertip.

Leave to cool in the tin for 10 minutes then invert the tin on to a wire rack, remove the tin and lining paper and leave to cool completely. Cut into 20 pieces and serve warm with whipped cream. This is best eaten on the day it is made.

For apricot & cranberry upside down cakes, spoon cranberry sauce over the base of the tin instead of the apricot jam. Cover with a 425 g (14 oz) can apricot halves, drained and arranged in rows, instead of the fresh fruit. Replace the lime rind and juice from the cake mixture with the grated rind of 1 orange. Top the fruit with the cake mixture and bake as above.

prune & sunflower squares

Cuts into **16**
Preparation time **25 minutes**
Cooking time **30–35 minutes**

250 g (8 oz) **ready-to-eat stoned prunes**, roughly chopped
1 teaspoon **vanilla essence**
200 ml (7 fl oz) **water**
150 g (5 oz) **butter**
100 g (3½ oz) **caster sugar**
2 tablespoons **golden syrup**
100 g (3½ oz) **self-raising flour**
150 g (5 oz) **porridge oats**
40 g (1½ oz) **sunflower seeds**

To finish
3 tablespoons **porridge oats**
2 tablespoons **sunflower seeds**

Put the prunes, vanilla and water in a small saucepan. Simmer, uncovered, for 5 minutes until soft and pulpy and the water has been absorbed.

Heat the butter, sugar and syrup in a larger saucepan until melted. Stir in the flour, oats and seeds and mix until well combined.

Spoon three-quarters of the mixture into a 20 cm (8 inch) shallow square cake tin lined with nonstick baking paper (see page 11). Press into an even layer then cover with the cooked prunes. Sprinkle the remaining oat mixture over the top in a thin layer then decorate with the extra oats and sunflower seeds. Bake in a preheated oven, 180°C (350°F), Gas Mark 4, for 25–30 minutes until golden brown.

Leave to cool in the tin for 10 minutes then mark into 16 squares and leave to cool completely. Lift the flapjack out of the tin using the lining paper, peel off the paper and separate the squares. Store in an airtight tin for up to 3 days.

For date & apple squares, instead of using the prunes and vanilla, cook 150 g (5 oz) ready-chopped dates with 1 cored and chopped dessert apple in the same amount of water as above. Strain any excess liquid before spooning over the oat mixture. Continue the recipe as above.

chocolate caramel shortbread

Cuts into **15**
Preparation time **20 minutes,**
  plus chilling
Cooking time **15 minutes**

100 g (3½ oz) **butter,**
  at room temperature
50 g (2 oz) **caster sugar**
100 g (3½ oz) **brown rice flour**
100 g (3½ oz) **cornflour**

For the caramel
100 g (3½ oz) **butter**
50 g (2 oz) **soft light**
  brown sugar
397 g (13 oz) can **condensed**
  milk

For the topping
100 g (3½ oz) **white**
  chocolate, broken into
  pieces
100 g (3½ oz) **plain dark**
  chocolate, broken into
  pieces

Beat the butter and sugar together in a mixing bowl until pale and creamy, then stir in the flours until well combined. Press the shortbread into a 28 x 18 cm (11 x 7 inch) baking tin, then place in a preheated oven, 200°C (400°F), Gas Mark 6, for 10–12 minutes until golden.

Meanwhile, place the caramel ingredients in a heavy-based saucepan and heat over a low heat until the sugar has dissolved, then cook for 5 minutes, stirring continuously until just beginning to darken. Remove from the heat and leave to cool a little, then pour the caramel over the shortbread base and leave to cool completely.

Melt the white and dark chocolate in separate heatproof bowls set over saucepans of simmering water. When the caramel is firm, spoon alternate spoonfuls of the white and dark chocolate over the caramel, tap the tin on the work surface so that the different chocolates merge, then use a knife to make swirls in the chocolate. Refrigerate until set, then cut into 15 pieces.

For caramel pine nut slice, make the shortbread base as above, adding the grated rind of ½ orange along with the flour. Bake as above. Stir 50 g (2 oz) pine nuts into the caramel just before pouring over the shortbread. When cool, decorate with 100 g (3½ oz) melted dark chocolate drizzled randomly over the top so that the caramel can still be seen.

centrepiece
cakes

strawberry macaroon cake

Cuts into **8**
Preparation time **40 minutes**
Cooking time **35–45 minutes**

4 **egg whites**
¼ teaspoon **cream of tartar**
125 g (4 oz) **light muscovado sugar**
100 g (3½ oz) **caster sugar**
1 teaspoon **white wine vinegar**
50 g (2 oz) **walnut pieces**, lightly toasted and chopped

For the filling
200 ml (7 fl oz) **double cream**
250 g (8 oz) **strawberries**

Whisk the egg whites and cream of tartar in a large clean bowl until stiff. Combine the sugars then gradually whisk into the egg white, a little at a time, until it has all been added. Whisk for a few minutes more until the meringue mixture is thick and glossy. Fold in the walnuts.

Divide the meringue mixture evenly between 2 greased 20 cm (8 inch) sandwich tins, base-lined with nonstick baking paper. Spread the surfaces level then swirl the tops with the back of a spoon. Bake in a preheated oven, 150°C (300°F), Gas Mark 2, for 35–45 minutes until lightly browned and crisp. Loosen the edges and leave to cool in the tins.

Re-loosen the edges of the meringues and turn out on to 2 clean tea towels. Peel off the lining paper then put one of the meringues on a serving plate.

Whip the cream until softly peaking then spoon three-quarters over the meringue. Halve 8 of the smallest strawberries and set aside. Hull and slice the rest and arrange on the cream. Cover with the second meringue, top uppermost. Decorate with spoonfuls of the remaining cream and the reserved halved strawberries. Serve within 2 hours of assembly.

For chocolate & chestnut macaroon cake, fold 2 tablespoons cocoa powder into the meringue mixture just before adding the nuts. Bake as above then replace the strawberries and cream filling with 150 ml (¼ pint) double cream, whipped and folded with a 220 g (7½ oz) can sweetened chestnut purée. Decorate the top with chocolate curls.

chocolate & rum cake

Cuts into **16**
Preparation time **15 minutes**
Cooking time **25–30 minutes**

150 g (5 oz) **plain dark chocolate**, broken into pieces
grated rind and juice of
  1 orange
a few drops of **rum essence** (optional)
150 g (5 oz) **unsalted butter**, at room temperature
150 g (5 oz) **caster sugar**
4 **eggs**, separated
150 g (5 oz) **ground almonds**

For the chocolate icing
150 g (5 oz) **plain dark chocolate**, broken into pieces
100 g (3½ oz) **unsalted butter**

To decorate
8–16 **crystallized violet petals**, (optional)

Melt together the chocolate, orange rind and juice and rum essence, if using, in a heatproof bowl set over a saucepan of gently simmering water.

Place the butter and all but 1 tablespoon of the sugar in a large mixing bowl and beat together until pale and creamy. Beat in the egg yolks, one at a time, then stir in the melted chocolate.

Whisk the egg whites in a large clean bowl until softly peaking. Add the remaining sugar, then whisk until stiff. Fold the egg whites into the chocolate mixture with the ground almonds, then spoon into 2 greased and base-lined 20 cm (8 inch) sandwich tins.

Bake in a preheated oven, 180°C (350°F), Gas Mark 4, for 20–25 minutes, until the sides of the cakes are cooked but the centres are still a little unset. Remove from the oven, leave to cool in the tins for a few minutes then turn out gently on to a wire rack.

Ice the cake. Melt the chocolate as before then whisk in the butter, a tablespoon at a time, until melted. Remove from the heat and whisk occasionally until cool. If the icing is runny, put the bowl in the refrigerator until it firms up a little. Fill and ice the cooled cake with the chocolate mixture. Decorate with crystallized violet petals, if liked.

For orange liqueur cake, omit the rum. Make the cake as above, then sandwich and top it with 200 ml (7 fl oz) whipped double cream flavoured with 2 tablespoons Cointreau and 2 tablespoons icing sugar. Decorate with fresh orange segments.

apple sauce cake

Cuts into **8**
Preparation time **30 minutes**
Cooking time **40–45 minutes**

2 **cooking apples**, about
   250 g (8 oz) each, cored,
   peeled and thinly sliced
2 tablespoons **water**
a little **lemon juice**
250 g (8 oz) **white bread**
   flour
2½ teaspoons **baking powder**
1 teaspoon **ground cinnamon**
½ teaspoon **ground ginger**
¼ teaspoon **grated nutmeg**
150 g (5 oz) **reduced-fat**
   spread
175 g (6 oz) **caster sugar**
3 **eggs**, beaten

Put half the apple slices in a small saucepan with the water, then cover and simmer for 5 minutes until pulpy. Put the remaining apple slices in a bowl of cold water with a little lemon juice.

Mix the flour, baking powder, half the ground cinnamon and all of the ginger and nutmeg together in a mixing bowl.

Cream the reduced-fat spread with 150 g (5 oz) of the sugar in another bowl. Gradually mix in alternate spoonfuls of beaten egg and flour mixture until all has been added and the mixture is smooth. Stir in the cooked apple.

Pour the mixture into a lightly oiled 23 cm (9 inch) spring-form cake tin and spread the surface level. Drain the remaining apples well and arrange the slices in rings on top of the cake mixture. Sprinkle with the remaining sugar and cinnamon. Bake in a preheated oven, 180°C (350°F), Gas Mark 4, for 35–40 minutes until well risen and a skewer inserted into the centre comes out clean.

Serve the cake while still warm, on its own or as a pudding with crème fraîche, yogurt or custard.

For spiced pear cake, make the cake replacing the apples with the same weight of pears, 1 teaspoon ground ginger and ½ teaspoon ground cinnamon, sprinkling half the ginger on the top of the cake with the sugar. Bake as above.

chocolate & sweet potato torte

Cuts into **12–14**
Preparation time **40 minutes**
Cooking time **40–45 minutes**

200 g (7 oz) **self-raising flour**
50 g (2 oz) **cocoa powder**
1 teaspoon **bicarbonate of soda**
175 g (6 oz) **butter**
175 g (6 oz) **light muscovado sugar**
3 **eggs**, beaten
400 g (13 oz) **sweet potato**, boiled, drained and mashed with 3 tablespoons **milk**
40 g (1½ oz) chopped **crystallized or glacé ginger**

For the frosting
150 g (5 oz) **plain dark chocolate**
2 tablespoons **light muscovado sugar**
200 ml (7 fl oz) **full-fat crème fraîche**

To decorate
25 g (1 oz) chopped **crystallized or glacé ginger**
a few **crystallized rose petals or violets** (see page 144)

Mix the flour, cocoa powder and bicarbonate of soda together in a bowl. Beat the butter and sugar together in a mixing bowl until pale and creamy. Gradually mix in alternate spoonfuls of beaten egg and flour mixture until all has been added and the mixture is smooth. Stir in the mashed sweet potato and ginger.

Pour the mixture into a 23 cm (9 inch) spring-form tin, greased and base-lined with oiled greaseproof paper, then spread the surface level. Bake in a preheated oven, 160°C (325°F), Gas Mark 3, for 45–50 minutes until the cake has risen with a slightly domed and cracked top and a skewer inserted into the centre comes out clean.

Leave to cool in the tin for 15 minutes (don't worry if it sinks slightly) then turn out on to a wire rack and peel off the lining paper. Leave to cool completely.

Make the frosting. Melt the chocolate and muscovado sugar in a heatproof bowl set over a saucepan of gently simmering water. Remove from the heat, add the crème fraîche and stir until smooth and glossy. Chill for 10–30 minutes if needed, until the frosting is thick enough to spread. Spoon the chocolate frosting over the cake top and sides and swirl with a knife.

Sprinkle with the ginger and crystallized flower petals, if using, then leave in a cool place to set.

lemon angel food cake

Cuts into **8**
Preparation time **30 minutes**
Cooking time **25–30 minutes**

50 g (2 oz) **plain flour**
finely grated rind of ½ **lemon**
6 **egg whites**
pinch of **salt**
¾ teaspoon **cream of tartar**
200 g (7 oz) **caster sugar**
crystallized rose petals or
   flowers, to decorate
   (optional)

For the topping
150 g (5 oz) **lemon curd**
125 ml (4 fl oz) **soured cream**

Sift the flour into a bowl, stir in the lemon rind and set aside.

Whisk the egg whites, salt and cream of tartar in a large clean bowl until stiff but moist-looking. Gradually whisk in the sugar, a tablespoonful at a time, until it has all been added. Whisk for a few minutes more until the meringue mixture is thick and glossy.

Gently fold in the flour mixture using a metal spoon and a swirling figure-of-eight action. Pour into a 20 or 23 cm (8 or 9 inch) nonstick angel cake tin. Bake in a preheated oven, 190°C (375°F), Gas Mark 5, for 25–30 minutes until well risen, the cake is golden and springs back when gently pressed with a fingertip.

Invert the tin on to a wire rack and leave to cool. As it cools the cake will fall out of the tin. When cold, mix the lemon curd and soured cream together and spread over the top of the cake. Sprinkle with crystallized rose petals or flowers, if using.

To crystallize flowers such as rose petals or viola, pansy or herb flowers, first make sure they are clean. Brush them with egg white then dust lightly with a little caster sugar. Leave to dry for at least 30 minutes before using to decorate the cake.

For lime angel food cake with pistachios, replace the grated lemon rind with the finely grated rind of 1 lime and use lime curd in place of the lemon curd for the topping. Toast 25 g (1 oz) pistachio nuts with 1 tablespoon caster sugar under a grill until the sugar has dissolved and caramelized lightly, cool, then roughly chop and sprinkle over the cake.

144

plum & almond streusel cake

Cuts into **12**

Preparation time **35 minutes**

Cooking time **1 hour–1 hour 10 minutes**

For the streusel topping
25 g (1 oz) **self-raising flour**
25 g (1 oz) **caster sugar**
25 g (1 oz) **butter**, diced
40 g (1½ oz) **flaked almonds**

For the cake
175 g (6 oz) **butter**, at room temperature
175 g (6 oz) **caster sugar**
3 **eggs**, beaten
175 g (6 oz) **self-raising flour**
1 teaspoon **baking powder**
50 g (2 oz) **ground almonds**
½ teaspoon **almond essence**
400 g (13 oz) **red plums**, halved, stoned and thickly sliced
sifted **icing sugar**, to decorate

Make the streusel topping. Put the flour and sugar in a small bowl. Add the butter and rub in with your fingertips until the mixture resembles fine breadcrumbs. Stir in the flaked almonds.

Make the cake. Beat the butter and sugar together in a mixing bowl until pale and creamy. Gradually mix in alternate spoonfuls of beaten egg and flour until all has been added. Stir in the baking powder, ground almonds and almond essence.

Spoon the cake mixture into a 23 cm (9 inch) spring-form tin lined with nonstick baking paper over base and sides, and spread the surface level. Arrange the sliced plums randomly over the top then sprinkle with the streusel topping.

Bake in a preheated oven, 180°C (350°F), Gas Mark 4, for 1 hour–1 hour 10 minutes, or until a skewer inserted into the centre comes out clean, covering the cake loosely with foil halfway during cooking if the top appears to be browning too quickly.

Leave to cool in the tin for 15 minutes then remove the tin and leave the cake to cool completely. When ready to serve, remove the lining paper and transfer to a serving plate. Dust with sifted icing sugar. Cut into wedges and serve plain or serve while still warm as a pudding with a spoonful of whipped cream or vanilla ice cream. Eat within 2 days.

For peach melba streusel cake, follow the basic recipe above but replace the plums with 2 sliced fresh peaches and 100 g (3½ oz) raspberries.

cherub cake

Cuts into **8**
Preparation time **1½ hours,
    plus overnight drying**
Cooking time **1–1¼ hours**

175 g (6 oz) **soft margarine**
175 g (6 oz) **caster sugar**
3 **eggs**, beaten
250 g (8 oz) **self-raising flour**
finely grated rind of **2 limes**
juice of 1½ **limes**
100 g (3½ oz) **butter**, at room
    temperature
250 g (8 oz) **icing sugar**, plus
    extra for dusting
4 tablespoons **raspberry jam**
450 g (14½ oz) **ready-rolled
    white icing**
250 g (8 oz) **modelling icing**
edible **gold food colouring**
small tube **white writing icing**
    (optional)

Beat the margarine and sugar together in a bowl until pale and creamy. Mix in spoonfuls of the egg and flour until all has been added and the mixture is smooth.

Stir in the lime rind and the juice from ½ a lime. Spoon the mixture into a 20 cm (8 inch) deep round cake tin lined with nonstick baking paper and spread the surface level. Bake in a preheated oven, 160°C (325°F), Gas Mark 3, for 1–1¼ hours until well risen. Leave to cool in the tin then turn out. Peel off the lining paper and slice the cake horizontally into 3 layers.

Beat the butter, icing sugar and remaining lime juice together to make a smooth butter cream. Sandwich the cakes together using the butter cream and jam. Spread the remaining mix thinly over the cake top and sides.

Drape the rolled icing over the cake. Gently press over the top and sides until smooth and trim away the excess icing. Press a small piece of modelling icing into a 6 cm (2½ inch) nonstick cherub icing mould. Invert the mould and gently ease out the shaped cherub. Trim and make another 3 cherubs.

Roll out the remaining icing and cut into thin strips for the icing ribbons. Twist each one like a corkscrew over a wooden spoon handle and leave overnight to dry. Paint gold detail on the cherub wings. Arrange the cherubs on top of the cake, with the icing ribbons. Secure with writing icing.

apricot & orange swiss roll

Cuts into **8**
Preparation time **30 minutes**
Cooking time **18–20 minutes**

For the filling
200 g (7 oz) **ready-to-eat
  dried apricots**
200 ml (7 fl oz) **apple juice**

For the sponge
4 **eggs**
125 g (4 oz) **caster sugar**,
  plus extra for sprinkling
grated rind of 1 **orange**
125 g (4 oz) **plain flour**, sifted

Simmer the apricots and apple juice in a saucepan, covered, for 10 minutes or until most of the liquid has been absorbed. Purée then leave to cool.

Make the sponge. Put the eggs, sugar and orange rind in a large heatproof bowl set over a saucepan of gently simmering water. Whisk, using an electric whisk, for 5–10 minutes until very thick and foamy and the whisk leaves a trail when lifted above the mixture.

Gently fold in the sifted flour. Pour the mixture into a 30 x 23 cm (12 x 9 inch) roasting or a swiss roll tin lined with nonstick baking paper (see page 11), and ease into the corners. Bake in a preheated oven, 200°C (400°F), Gas Mark 6, for 8–10 minutes until the sponge is golden brown and just beginning to shrink away from the sides, and the top springs back when gently pressed with a fingertip.

Meanwhile, cover a clean damp tea towel with nonstick baking paper and sprinkle with a little caster sugar. Quickly turn out the cooked sponge on to the sugared paper. Carefully peel off the lining paper. Spread the apricot purée over the sponge then, starting with a short side and using the paper to help, roll up to form a log. Leave to cool and serve the same day.

For strawberry & almond roulade, sprinkle 40 g (1½ oz) flaked almonds over the paper-lined tin and flavour the sponge mixture with ½ teaspoon almond essence instead of orange rind. Fill the roulade with 6 tablespoons strawberry jam instead of the apricot purée and dust with sifted icing sugar.

chocolate truffle cake

Cuts into **8**
Preparation time **15 minutes**
Cooking time **40 minutes**

250 g (8 oz) **plain dark chocolate**, broken into pieces
125 g (4 oz) **unsalted butter**
50 ml (2 fl oz) **double cream**
4 **eggs**, separated
125 g (4 oz) **caster sugar**
2 tablespoons **cocoa powder**, sifted
icing sugar, for dusting

Melt the chocolate, butter and cream together in a heatproof bowl set over a saucepan of gently simmering water. Remove from the heat and leave to cool for 5 minutes.

Whisk the egg yolks with 75 g (3 oz) of the sugar until pale and stir in the cooled chocolate mixture.

Whisk the egg whites in a large clean bowl until softly peaking then whisk in the remaining sugar. Fold into the egg yolk mixture with the sifted cocoa powder until evenly incorporated.

Pour the cake mixture into an oiled and base-lined 23 cm (9 inch) spring-form cake tin that has been lightly dusted all over with a little extra cocoa powder. Bake in a preheated oven, 180°C (350°F), Gas Mark 4, for 35 minutes.

Leave to cool in the tin for 10 minutes then turn out on to a serving plate. Serve in wedges, while still warm, with whipped cream and strawberries.

For chocolate & orange cake with brandied oranges, add the finely grated rind of 1 orange when folding in the icing sugar above. Remove the rind from 3 oranges, cut them into segments and soak in 3 tablespoons brandy and 1 tablespoon clear honey. Serve the oranges with the cake and spoon over crème fraîche.

st clements cake

Cuts into **8**
Preparation time **30 minutes**
Cooking time **20 minutes**

175 g (6 oz) **soft margarine**
175 g (6 oz) **caster sugar**
175 g (6 oz) **self-raising flour**
1 teaspoon **baking powder**
3 eggs
finely grated rind of 1 **lemon**
finely grated rind of 1 **orange**
sifted **icing sugar**, for dusting

For the filling
3 tablespoons **lemon curd**
150 ml (¼ pint) **double cream**,
   whipped

Beat all of the cake ingredients in a mixing bowl or a food processor until smooth.

Spoon the cake mixture evenly into 2 greased and base-lined 18 cm (7 inch) sandwich tins and spread the surfaces level. Bake in a preheated oven, 180°C (350°F), Gas Mark 4, for 20 minutes until well risen, the cake is golden brown and springs back when gently pressed with a fingertip.

Leave to cool in the tin for 5 minutes then loosen the edges, turn out on to a wire rack and peel off the lining paper. Leave to cool.

Transfer one of the cakes to a serving plate and spread with the lemon curd. Spoon the whipped cream on top then cover with the remaining cake. Dust the top of the cake lightly with sifted icing sugar. This is best eaten on the day it is made.

For chocolate & vanilla cake, omit the lemon and orange rind from the cake mixture and replace 25 g (1 oz) of the flour with the same weight of cocoa powder. Bake as above then fill with 3 tablespoons chocolate spread instead of lemon curd and 150 ml (¼ pint) whipped double cream flavoured with 1 teaspoon vanilla essence.

chocolate & chestnut roulade

Cuts into **8**
Preparation time **20 minutes,
plus cooling**
Cooking time **25 minutes**

125 g (4 oz) **plain dark
  chocolate**
5 **eggs**, separated
175 g (6 oz) **caster sugar**,
  plus extra for sprinkling
2 tablespoons **cocoa powder**,
  sifted
icing sugar, for dusting

For the filling
250 g (8 oz) **unsweetened
  chestnut purée**
4 tablespoons **icing sugar**
2 tablespoons **brandy**
250 ml (8 fl oz) **double cream**

Melt the chocolate in a heatproof bowl set over a
saucepan of simmering water, stirring occasionally.
Remove from the heat and leave to cool for 5 minutes.

Put the egg yolks in a bowl, add the sugar and whisk
together for 5 minutes until pale and very thick. Stir in
the melted chocolate and the cocoa powder. Whisk
the egg whites in a large clean bowl until stiff then
fold into the chocolate mixture until evenly combined.

Transfer the mixture to an oiled and lined 33 x 23 cm
(13 x 9 inch) Swiss roll tin, easing it well into the
corners and spreading the surface level with a palette
knife. Bake in a preheated oven, 180°C (350°F), Gas
Mark 4, for 20 minutes until risen and set.

Meanwhile, cover a clean damp tea towel with
nonstick baking paper and sprinkle with a little caster
sugar. Quickly turn out the cooked sponge on to the
paper. Carefully peel off the lining paper and cover the
sponge with a clean tea towel. Leave to cool.

Make the filling. Blend the chestnut purée and icing
sugar in a food processor until smooth. Transfer to a
bowl and stir in the brandy. Slowly whisk in the cream
until light and fluffy. Spread the filling over the sponge,
leaving a 1 cm (½ inch) border all round. Starting with
a short side and using the paper to help, roll up the
sponge to form a log. Dust with icing sugar and serve.

chocolate & date sandwich cake

Cuts into **10**
Preparation time **30 minutes**
Cooking time **25 minutes**

150 g (5 oz) **ready-chopped dried dates**
150 ml (¼ pint) **boiling water**, plus 6 tablespoons
50 g (2 oz) **cocoa powder**
150 ml (¼ pint) **sunflower oil**
3 **eggs**
175 g (6 oz) **caster sugar**
175 g (6 oz) **self-raising flour**
1½ teaspoons **baking powder**

To finish
150 ml (¼ pint) **double cream**
150 g (5 oz) **fromage frais**
3 tablespoons **chocolate spread**
5 bought **chocolate truffles**, halved

Simmer the dates in a saucepan with the 150 ml (¼ pint) boiling water, covered, for 5 minutes until softened. Gradually mix the cocoa powder in a bowl with the remaining 6 tablespoons boiling water until smooth. Leave the dates and dissolved cocoa powder to cool.

Add the oil, eggs and sugar to the dissolved cocoa powder then whisk together until smooth. Add the flour and baking powder then whisk again. Stir in the cooled dates and any cooking liquid and mix well.

Divide the mixture evenly between 2 x 20 cm (8 inch) sandwich tins, greased and base-lined with oiled greaseproof paper, and spread the surfaces level. Bake in a preheated oven, 180°C (350°F), Gas Mark 4, for 20 minutes until well risen and the cakes spring back when gently pressed with a fingertip.

Leave to cool in the tins for 5 minutes then loosen the edges, turn out on to a wire rack and peel off the lining paper. Leave to cool completely.

Whip the cream until softly peaking then fold in the fromage frais. Put one cake on to a serving plate, spoon over chocolate spread then half the cream. Top with the second cake and spread with the remaining cream. Decorate with the halved chocolate truffles.

For black forest cake, make the cake as above but omit the dates. Drizzle each cooked cake with 2 tablespoons kirsch then fill with the whipped cream and fromage frais, adding drained, stoned black cherries from a can to the middle and top of the cake.

coffee cake with pistachio praline

Cuts into **12**
Preparation time **40 minutes**
Cooking time **30–35 minutes**

6 eggs
175 g (6 oz) **caster sugar**
175 g (6 oz) **plain flour**, sifted
50 g (2 oz) **unsalted butter**,
    melted
2 tablespoons ready-made
    espresso coffee, cooled

For the praline
65 g (2½ oz) **shelled
    pistachio nuts**
125 g (4 oz) **granulated
    sugar**
50 ml (2 fl oz) **water**

For the maple syrup icing
6 **egg yolks**
175 g (6 oz) **caster sugar**
150 ml (¼ pint) **milk**
375 g (12 oz) **unsalted
    butter**, at room temperature,
    diced
3 tablespoons **maple syrup**

Whisk the eggs and sugar in a heatproof bowl set over a saucepan of gently simmering water for 5 minutes until very thick and the whisk leaves a trail when lifted above the mixture. Remove from the heat then fold in the flour, butter and coffee.

Transfer the mixture to an oiled and base-lined 23 cm (9 inch) cake tin and bake in a preheated oven, 180°C (350°F), Gas Mark 4, for 25–30 minutes. Leave to cool in the tin for 5 minutes then turn out on to a wire rack. Slice the cake horizontally into 3 layers.

Put the nuts on a baking sheet. Heat the sugar and water in a heavy-based saucepan until the sugar dissolves. Increase the heat until the sugar turns light golden. Remove from the heat and pour over the nuts. Once set, break the praline into small pieces and then grind to a rough powder.

Beat the egg yolks and sugar together until pale. Heat the milk until just boiling, then whisk into the egg mixture. Return to the pan and heat gently, stirring, until the mixture coats the back of the spoon. Beat the mixture off the heat for 2–3 minutes and then gradually beat in the butter, a little at a time, until the mixture is thick and glossy. Beat in the maple syrup.

Fold half the praline into half the icing and use to sandwich the layers together. Spread the remaining icing over the top and sides of the cake and sprinkle with the reserved praline.

For chocolate cake with hazelnut praline, substitute 25 g (1 oz) of the flour for cocoa powder and use shelled hazelnuts in place of the pistachios.

blueberry meringue roulade

Cuts into **8**

Preparation time **30 minutes,
plus cooling**

Cooking time **15 minutes**

4 **egg whites**

250 g (8 oz) **caster sugar**,
plus extra for sprinkling

1 teaspoon **white wine
vinegar**

1 teaspoon **cornflour**

For the filling

grated rind of 1 **lime**

300 ml (½ pint) **double
cream**, whipped

150 g (5 oz) **blueberries**

3 **passion fruit**, halved

Whisk the egg whites in a large clean bowl until stiff. Gradually whisk in the sugar, a teaspoonful at time, until it has all been added. Whisk for a few minutes more until the meringue mixture is thick and glossy.

Combine the vinegar and cornflour then whisk into the meringue mixture. Spoon into a 33 x 23 cm (13 x 9 inch) Swiss roll tin lined with nonstick baking paper that stands a little above the top of the tin sides, then spread the surface level. Bake in a preheated oven, 190°C (375°F), Gas Mark 5, for 10 minutes until biscuit coloured and well risen, then reduce the heat to 160°C (325°F), Gas Mark 3, for 5 minutes until just firm to the touch and the top is slightly cracked.

Meanwhile, cover a clean tea towel with nonstick baking paper and sprinkle with a little caster sugar. Turn out the meringue on to the paper. Remove the tin. Leave to cool for 1–2 hours. Carefully peel off the lining paper.

Fold the lime rind into the whipped cream. Spread over the meringue then sprinkle with the blueberries and passion fruit seeds. Starting with a short side and using the paper to help, roll up the meringue to form a log. Serve the same day.

For minted strawberry roulade, spread the meringue with whipped cream folded with a small bunch of freshly chopped mint and 250 g (8 oz) roughly chopped strawberries. Make the roulade as above and decorate with halved baby strawberries and mint leaves dusted with sifted icing sugar.

family chocolate cake

Cuts into **8**
Preparation time **20 minutes, plus chilling**
Cooking time **30 minutes**

125 g (4 oz) **caster sugar**
4 **eggs**
100 g (3½ oz) **self-raising flour**
25 g (1 oz) **cocoa powder**
40 g (1½ oz) **unsalted butter**, melted
1 teaspoon **vanilla extract**

For the icing
375 g (12 oz) **plain dark chocolate**, broken into pieces
250 g (8 oz) **unsalted butter**
100 g (3½ oz) **icing sugar**, sifted

Put the sugar and eggs in a heatproof bowl set over a saucepan of gently simmering water. Whisk, using an electric whisk, for 5–10 minutes until very thick and foamy and the whisk leaves a trail when lifted above the mixture.

Sift over the flour and cocoa powder and carefully fold into the mixture with the melted butter and vanilla until well combined.

Pour the mixture into an oiled and base-lined 20 cm (8 inch) spring-form cake tin and bake in a preheated oven, 180°C (350°F), Gas Mark 4, for 25 minutes until risen and firm to the touch. Remove from the oven and leave to cool in the tin for 5 minutes. Turn out on to a wire rack and leave to cool.

Make the icing. Melt the chocolate and butter together in a heatproof bowl set over a saucepan of gently simmering water. Remove from the heat and beat in the icing sugar. Set aside to cool and then chill for 1 hour until thickened. Beat until pale and fluffy.

Slice the cake in half horizontally and use half of the icing to sandwich the halves back together. Use the remaining icing to cover the top and sides of the cake, swirling the mixture with a palette knife.

For chocolate orange cake, add the finely grated rind of 1 orange to the sugar and eggs when whisking and continue as above. Decorate the iced cake with curls of orange rind.

old-fashioned coffee cake

Cuts into **8**
Preparation time **30 minutes**
Cooking time **20 minutes**

175 g (6 oz) **soft margarine**
175 g (6 oz) **light muscovado or caster sugar**
175 g (6 oz) **self-raising flour**
1 teaspoon **baking powder**
3 **eggs**
3 teaspoons **instant coffee**, dissolved in 2 teaspoons boiling water

For the frosting
75 g (3 oz) **butter**, at room temperature
150 g (5 oz) **icing sugar**, sifted
3 teaspoons **instant coffee**, dissolved in 2 teaspoons boiling water
50 g (2 oz) **dark chocolate**, melted

Beat all of the cake ingredients in a mixing bowl or a food processor until smooth.

Divide the mixture evenly between 2 x 18 cm (7 inch) sandwich tins, greased and base-lined with oiled greaseproof paper, and spread the surfaces level. Bake in a preheated oven, 180°C (350°F), Gas Mark 4, for 20 minutes until well risen, the cakes are browned and spring back when gently pressed with a fingertip.

Leave the cakes for a few minutes then loosen the edges, turn out on to a wire rack and peel off the lining paper. Leave to cool.

Make the frosting. Put the butter and half the icing sugar in a mixing bowl, add the dissolved coffee and beat until smooth. Gradually mix in the remaining icing sugar until pale and creamy.

Put one of the cakes on a serving plate, spread with half the frosting then cover with the second cake. Spread the remaining frosting over the top. Pipe or drizzle swirls of melted chocolate on top. This cake can be stored in a cake tin for 2–3 days in a cool place.

For cinnamon & hazelnut cake, replace the dissolved coffee in the cake mixture with 1 teaspoon ground cinnamon and 50 g (2 oz) toasted chopped hazelnuts. Use the maple frosting on page 168 to fill and cover the cake. Sprinkle with roughly chopped hazelnuts and dust with ground cinnamon to finish.

carrot & walnut cake

Cuts into **10**
Preparation time **40 minutes**
Cooking time **25 minutes**

150 ml (¼ pint) **sunflower oil**
3 **eggs**
175 g (6 oz) **light muscovado sugar**
175 g (6 oz) **self-raising flour**
1½ teaspoons **baking powder**
grated rind of ½ **orange**
1 teaspoon **ground cinnamon**
150 g (5 oz) **carrots**, coarsely grated
50 g (2 oz) **walnuts**, finely chopped

For the maple frosting
250 ml (8 fl oz) **maple syrup**
2 **egg whites**
pinch of **salt**

To decorate
5 **walnut halves**, halved

Put the oil, eggs and sugar in a mixing bowl and whisk together until smooth.

Add the flour, baking powder, orange rind and ground cinnamon and whisk again until smooth. Stir in the grated carrots and chopped nuts. Divide the mixture between 2 x 20 cm (8 inch) sandwich tins, greased and base-lined with oiled greaseproof paper, and level.

Bake in a preheated oven, 180°C (350°F), Gas Mark 4, for about 20 minutes until the tops spring back when pressed. Cool for 5 minutes, then turn out on to a wire rack and peel off the lining paper. Leave to cool.

Make the maple frosting. Pour the maple syrup into a saucepan and heat to 115°C (240°F) on a sugar thermometer. As the temperature begins to rise, whisk the egg whites and salt in a clean bowl until stiff. When the syrup is ready, whisk it into the egg whites in a thin trickle until the frosting is like a meringue mixture. Keep whisking for a few minutes more until very thick.

Cut each cake in half then sandwich 4 layers together with frosting. Transfer to a serving plate, then swirl the rest of the frosting over the top and sides of the cake. Decorate the top with the walnut pieces.

For spiced apple cake with calvados cream, make the cake omitting the orange rind, carrots and walnuts. Add 200 g (7 oz) peeled, cored and coarsely grated cooking apples instead. Bake as above, then sandwich with 150 ml (¼ pint) double cream, whipped and folded with 2 tablespoons calvados and 2 tablespoons runny honey. Dust the top with icing sugar.

victoria sandwich cake

Cuts into **8**
Preparation time **20 minutes**
Cooking time **20 minutes**

175 g (6 oz) **butter**, at room
   temperature
175 g (6 oz) **caster sugar**
175 g (6 oz) **brown rice flour**
3 **eggs**
1 tablespoon **baking powder**
a few drops of **vanilla
   essence**
1 tablespoon **milk**

To decorate
4 tablespoons **raspberry jam**
sifted icing sugar, for dusting

Place all the cake ingredients in a mixing bowl or a
food processor and beat well until smooth.

Divide the mixture evenly between 2 greased and
floured 18 cm (7 inch) nonstick round cake tins and
bake in a preheated oven, 200°C (400°F), Gas Mark
6, for about 20 minutes until golden and risen.

Remove from the oven and turn out on to a wire rack
to cool. Sandwich the cakes together with the jam and
dust with icing sugar.

For chocolate birthday cake, make the cakes above,
replacing 1 tablespoon rice flour with cocoa powder.
Make a chocolate icing by dissolving 2 tablespoons
cocoa powder in 2 tablespoons boiling water and
leaving to cool. Beat together 375 g (12 oz) icing
sugar and 175 g (6 oz) softened butter until pale and
fluffy, then beat in the dissolved cocoa. Use to fill
and cover the cake.

chocolate guinness cake

Cuts into **10**
Preparation time **40 minutes**,
    plus standing and chilling
Cooking time **45–55 minutes**

125 g (4 oz) **butter**, at room
    temperature
250 g (8 oz) **light muscovado
    sugar**
175 g (6 oz) **plain flour**
50 g (2 oz) **cocoa powder**
½ teaspoon **baking powder**
1 teaspoon **bicarbonate of
    soda**
3 **eggs**, beaten
200 ml (7 fl oz) **Guinness** or
    other stout
25 g (1 oz) **white chocolate
    curls**, to decorate
sifted **cocoa powder**,
    for dusting

**For the white chocolate
frosting**
200 ml (7 fl oz) **double cream**
200 g (7 oz) **white chocolate**,
    broken into pieces

Cream the butter and sugar together in a mixing bowl
until pale and creamy. Sift the flour, cocoa, baking
powder and bicarbonate of soda into a bowl. Gradually
beat in alternate spoonfuls of egg, flour mixture and
Guinness until all have been added and the mixture
is smooth.

Spoon into a 20 cm (8 inch) spring-form tin, greased
and base-lined with oiled greaseproof paper, and spread
the surface level. Bake in a preheated oven, 160°C
(325°F), Gas Mark 3, for 45–55 minutes until well risen,
the top is slightly cracked and a skewer inserted into
the centre comes out clean. Leave to cool in the tin for
10 minutes then loosen the edges, turn out on to a wire
rack and peel off the lining paper.

Make the white chocolate frosting. Bring half the cream
just to the boil in a small saucepan, then remove from
the heat. Add the chocolate, set aside for 10 minutes
until melted. Stir then chill for 15 minutes. Whip the
remaining cream then whisk in the chocolate cream
until thick. Chill for another 15 minutes.

Transfer the cake to a serving plate and spoon the
chocolate cream over the top. Decorate with chocolate
curls and dust with sifted cocoa powder.

cherry & orange roulade

Cuts into **8**
Preparation time **30 minutes, plus cooling**
Cooking time **20 minutes**

5 large **eggs**, separated
250 g (8 oz) **caster sugar**, plus extra for dusting
100 g (3½ oz) **plain flour**, sifted
grated rind of 1½ **oranges**
40 g (1½ oz) **flaked almonds**
300 g (10 oz) **low-fat cream cheese**
425 g (14 oz) can **stoned black cherries**, drained
a few **fresh cherries** (optional)

Put the egg yolks and 175 g (6 oz) of the sugar in a large heatproof bowl set over a saucepan of gently simmering water. Whisk until very thick and pale. Remove from the heat and gently fold in the sifted flour and the rind from 1 orange. Whisk the egg whites in a large clean bowl until stiff but moist-looking. Fold a large spoonful into the yolk mixture to loosen it slightly, then gently fold in the rest.

Pour the mixture into a 30 x 23 cm (12 x 9 inch) baking tin lined with nonstick baking paper, and ease into the corners. Sprinkle with the flaked almonds and bake in a preheated oven, 180°F (350°F), Gas Mark 4, for 15 minutes until the roulade is well risen and the top feels spongy. Remove from the oven and leave to cool.

Beat the cream cheese with the remaining orange rind and half the remaining sugar.

Cover a clean damp tea towel with nonstick baking paper and sprinkle with the remaining sugar. Turn out the roulade on to the paper. Peel off the lining paper.

Spread the cream cheese mixture over the top. Sprinkle with the canned cherries then, starting with a short side and using the paper to help, roll up the roulade. Transfer to a serving plate, add fresh cherries, if using, and cut into thick slices to serve.

For passion fruit and mango gâteau, make the sponge omitting the orange rind and bake as above. When cooked, cut into three strips widthways. Sandwich and top strips with 300 ml (½ pint) whipped double cream, the peeled, stoned and diced flesh of 1 mango and the pulp from 3 passion fruit.

lemon polenta cake

Cuts into **8–10**
Preparation time **20 minutes**
Cooking time **30 minutes**

125 g (4 oz) **plain flour**
1½ teaspoons **baking powder**
125 g (4 oz) **polenta**
3 **eggs**, plus 2 **egg whites**
175 g (6 oz) **golden caster sugar**
grated rind and juice of 2 **lemons**
100 ml (3½ fl oz) **vegetable oil**
150 ml (¼ pint) **buttermilk**

For the red wine strawberries
300 ml (½ pint) **red wine**
1 **vanilla pod**, split
150 g (5 oz) **caster sugar**
2 tablespoons **balsamic vinegar**
250 g (8 oz) **strawberries**, hulled

Sift the flour and baking powder into a mixing bowl. Stir in the polenta and set aside.

Whisk the eggs, egg whites and sugar together in another bowl, using an electric whisk, for 3–4 minutes until pale and very thick. Fold in the polenta mixture, lemon rind and juice, vegetable oil and buttermilk to form a smooth batter.

Pour the mixture into a greased and base-lined 25 cm (10 inch) spring-form cake tin. Bake in a preheated oven, 180°C (350°F), Gas Mark 4, for 30 minutes until risen and firm to the touch. Leave to cool in the tin for 10 minutes then loosen the edges, turn out on to a wire rack and peel off the lining paper. Leave to cool.

Meanwhile, prepare the red wine strawberries. Put the wine, vanilla pod and sugar in a saucepan and heat gently to dissolve the sugar. Increase the heat and simmer for 10–15 minutes until reduced and syrupy. Leave to cool then stir in the balsamic vinegar and strawberries.

Cut the cake into slices and serve as a dessert with the strawberries and their syrup.

For lemon drizzle cake, omit the red wine accompaniment. Make the cake as above. Heat the finely grated zest and juice of 2 lemons in a saucepan with 200 g (7 oz) caster sugar and 2 tablespoons water, until the sugar has just dissolved. Turn the cooked cake out on to a plate and spoon the hot syrup over the top. Leave it to cool and to absorb the syrup. Serve cut into wedges with whipped double cream.

chocolate & hazelnut gâteau

Cuts into **8–10**
Preparation time **30 minutes,
 plus chilling**
Cooking time **1–1¼ hours**

5 **eggs**, separated
300 g (10 oz) **caster sugar**
1 tablespoon **cornflour**
125 g (4 oz) **blanched
 hazelnuts**, toasted and
 finely ground
cocoa powder, for dusting

For the filling
250 g (8 oz) **plain dark
 chocolate**, broken into
 pieces
200 ml (7 fl oz) **double cream**

**For the chocolate
 hazelnuts**
50 g (2 oz) **hazelnuts**
50 g (2 oz) **plain dark
 chocolate**, melted

Whisk the egg whites in a large clean bowl until stiff. Whisk in the sugar, a tablespoonful at time, until it has all been added. Whisk again until the meringue mixture is thick and glossy. Fold in the cornflour and ground hazelnuts then spoon the mixture into a large piping bag fitted with a 1 cm (½ inch) plain piping tube.

Draw a 23 cm (9 inch) circle on 3 sheets of nonstick baking paper. Starting in the centre of each prepared circle, pipe the mixture in a continuous coil, finishing just within the outer line. Bake all 3 in a preheated oven, 150°C (300°F), Gas Mark 2, for 1–1¼ hours until lightly golden and dried out. Remove from the oven and transfer to a wire rack to cool completely.

Heat the chocolate and cream in a heatproof bowl set over a saucepan of simmering water, stirring until the chocolate has melted. Remove from the heat and leave to cool then chill for 1 hour until thickened.

Make the chocolate hazelnuts. Using a fork, dip the hazelnuts into the melted chocolate until coated. Leave to set on baking paper.

Beat the chocolate filling until light and fluffy and use it to sandwich the 3 meringue layers together. Decorate with the chocolate hazelnuts and serve dusted with cocoa powder.

For apricot & almond dacquiose, replace the hazelnuts with ground almonds. For the filling, cover 175 g (6 oz) ready-to-eat dried apricots with water and cook in a saucepan for 10 minutes. Purée until smooth, cool, then fold into 300 ml (½ pint) whipped double cream.

cut-&-come-again cakes

pepper cake

Cuts into **10**
Preparation time **25 minutes, plus cooling**
Cooking time **45–55 minutes**

125 g (4 oz) **butter**
125 g (4 oz) **raisins**
125 g (4 oz) **currants**
75 g (3 oz) **sultanas**
150 g (5 oz) **light muscovado sugar**
150 ml (¼ pint) **water**
300 g (10 oz) **self-raising flour**
1 teaspoon **peppercorns**, coarsely crushed
1 teaspoon **whole cloves**, coarsely crushed
1 teaspoon **ground ginger**
2 **eggs**

Put the butter, dried fruit, sugar and water in a saucepan and bring to the boil. Heat gently for 5 minutes then leave to cool for 15 minutes.

Put the flour, crushed peppercorns, crushed cloves and ginger in a mixing bowl. Add the fruit mixture and eggs and mix to a soft dropping consistency.

Spoon into a 20 cm (8 inch) spring-form tin, greased and base-lined with oiled greaseproof paper. Spread the surface level then bake in a preheated oven, 160°C (325°F), Gas Mark 3, for 45–55 minutes until well risen, the top is slightly cracked and a skewer inserted into the centre comes out clean. (If you have a fan-assisted oven, you may need to cover the top of the cake lightly with foil after 30 minutes to prevent the top from overbrowning.)

Leave to cool for 10 minutes then loosen the edges, turn out on to a wire rack and peel off the lining paper. Leave to cool completely. Store in an airtight tin for up to 3 days.

For light farmhouse fruit cake, follow the recipe above but omit the peppercorns, whole cloves and ground ginger and add 1 teaspoon mixed spice to the mixture instead.

banana, date & walnut loaf

Cuts into **10**
Preparation time **25 minutes**
Cooking time **1 hour 10 minutes–1¼ hours**

400 g (13 oz) **bananas**, weighed with skins on
1 tablespoon **lemon juice**
300 g (10 oz) **self-raising flour**
1 teaspoon **baking powder**
125 g (4 oz) **caster sugar**
125 g (4 oz) **butter**, melted
2 **eggs**, beaten
175 g (6 oz) **ready-chopped dried dates**
50 g (2 oz) **walnut pieces**

To decorate
walnut halves
banana chips

Peel then mash the bananas with the lemon juice.

Put the flour, baking powder and sugar in a mixing bowl. Add the mashed bananas, melted butter and eggs and mix together. Stir in the dates and walnut pieces then spoon into a greased 1 kg (2 lb) loaf tin, its base and 2 long sides also lined with oiled greaseproof paper. Spread the surface level and decorate the top with walnut halves and banana chips, if using.

Bake in the centre of a preheated oven, 160°C (325°F), Gas Mark 3, for 1 hour 10 minutes–1¼ hours until well risen, the top has cracked and a skewer inserted into the centre comes out clean. Leave to cool for 10 minutes then loosen the edges, turn out on to a wire rack and peel off the lining paper. Leave to cool completely. Store in an airtight tin for up to 5 days.

For chocolate, cherry & apricot loaf, add 75 g (3 oz) each of diced dark chocolate, roughly chopped glacé cherries and diced ready-to-eat dried apricots instead of the dates and walnuts. Spoon into the loaf tin and bake as above. Drizzle the top of the cooled cake with 75 g (3 oz) melted dark chocolate.

jamaican ginger cake

Cuts into **10**
Preparation time **30 minutes**
Cooking time **50–60 minutes**

150 g (5 oz) **butter**
150 g (5 oz) **golden syrup**
150 g (5 oz) **black treacle**
150 g (5 oz) **plain flour**
150 g (5 oz) **wholemeal bread flour**
4 teaspoons **ground ginger**
1 teaspoon **ground mixed spice**
1 teaspoon **bicarbonate of soda**
2 **eggs**, beaten
4 tablespoons **milk**

For the topping
1 tablespoon **apricot jam**
125 g (4 oz) **exotic dried fruit**, cut into strips
1 piece **stem ginger,** drained and sliced

Put the butter, syrup and treacle in a saucepan and heat gently, stirring occasionally until the butter has melted. Remove from the heat and cool for 5 minutes.

Mix all the dry ingredients together in a large mixing bowl. Gradually mix in the syrup mixture then the eggs and milk and beat well until smooth.

Pour into a greased 1 kg (2 lb) loaf tin, its base and 2 long sides also lined with oiled greaseproof paper. Bake in a preheated oven, 160°C (325°F), Gas Mark 3, for 50–60 minutes until well risen, the top has cracked and a skewer inserted into the centre comes out clean. Leave to cool in the tin for 10 minutes then loosen the edges and lift out of the tin using the lining paper. Transfer to a wire rack, peel off the lining paper and leave to cool.

Spread the top of the cake with the apricot jam, then decorate with strips of exotic dried fruit and ginger.

For parkin, make the ginger cake as above, replacing the wholemeal flour with 150 g (5 oz) medium oatmeal. Bake in a 20 cm (8 inch) square cake tin that has been lined with non-stick baking paper on the base and sides. Bake at 150°C (300°F), Gas Mark 2, for 50–60 minutes or until firm to the touch. When cool, turn out and wrap in greaseproof paper. Cut into 16 squares to serve.

whisky mac cake

Cuts into **24**
Preparation time **40 minutes,
plus overnight soaking**
Cooking time **3½–3¾ hours**

1 kg (2 lb) **luxury mixed
dried fruit**
4 tablespoons **whisky**
50 g (2 oz) **ready-chopped
glacé ginger**
grated rind and juice of 1
lemon
300 g (10 oz) **plain flour**
2 teaspoons **ground mixed
spice**
1 teaspoon **ground cinnamon**
250 g (8 oz) **butter**, at room
temperature
250 g (8 oz) **dark
muscovado sugar**
5 **eggs**, beaten
50 g (2 oz) **pecan nuts**,
roughly chopped

To decorate
11 **glace cherry halves**
11 **pecan nuts**

Put the dried fruit in a bowl with the whisky, glacé ginger, lemon rind and juice. Mix together, cover and leave to soak overnight.

Mix the flour with the spices. Beat the butter and sugar together in a mixing bowl until pale and creamy.

Mix in alternate spoonfuls of beaten egg and flour until all has been added and the mixture is smooth. Gradually mix in the soaked fruit and chopped nuts until evenly combined.

Spoon the mixture into a 20 cm (8 inch) deep round cake tin, base and sides lined with nonstick baking paper, and spread the surface level. Arrange the cherry halves and pecans around the top edge. Bake in the centre of a preheated oven, 140°C (275°F), Gas Mark 1, for 3½–3¾ hours or until a skewer inserted into the centre comes out clean. Leave to cool in the tin for 30 minutes then loosen the edges, turn out on to a wire rack and peel off the lining paper. Leave to cool completely. Decorate the cake with a strip of waxed paper tied round the cake with raffia, if liked. Store in an airtight tin for up to 2 weeks.

For rich fruit celebration cake, omit the whisky and soak the fruit in the grated rind and juice of 1 lemon and ½ orange. Omit the cherry and pecan topping and bake as above. When cold, place the cake on a cake board and brush the top and sides with 4 tablespoons sieved apricot jam. Cover with 450 g (14½ oz) thinly rolled marzipan, then 500 g (1 lb) ready-to-roll icing. Smooth the top and sides and trim off any excess. Decorate to suit the celebration.

cidered apple & fig loaf

Cuts into **10**

Preparation time **20 minutes,
plus soaking**

Cooking time **1 hour–1 hour
10 minutes**

300 ml (½ pint) **dry cider**

1 large **cooking apple**, about
300 g (10 oz) in total, cored,
peeled and chopped

175 g (6 oz) **ready-to-eat
dried figs**, chopped

150 g (5 oz) **caster sugar**

300 g (10 oz) **self-raising
flour**

2 **eggs**, beaten

1 tablespoon **sunflower
seeds**

1 tablespoon **pumpkin seeds**

Pour the cider into a saucepan, add the apple and figs
and bring to the boil. Simmer for 3–5 minutes until the
apples are just tender but still firm. Remove the pan
from the heat and leave to soak for 4 hours.

Mix the sugar, flour and eggs into the soaked fruit and
stir well.

Spoon into a greased 1 kg (2 lb) loaf tin, its base and
2 long sides also lined with oiled greaseproof paper
and spread the surface level. Sprinkle with the seeds
and bake in the centre of a preheated oven, 160°C
(325°F), Gas Mark 3, for 1 hour–1 hour 10 minutes
until well risen, the top has slightly cracked and a
skewer inserted into the centre comes out clean.

Leave to cool in the tin for 10 minutes then loosen
the edges and lift out of the tin using the lining paper.
Transfer to a wire rack, peel off the lining paper and
leave to cool completely. Serve cut into slices and
spread with a little butter. Store in an airtight tin for up
to 1 week.

For apple & mixed fruit loaf, cook the apple as
above in 300 ml (½ pint) apple juice instead of cider
with 175 g (6 oz) luxury mixed dried fruit instead of
dried figs. Continue as above, spooning the mixture
into the tin and sprinkling the top with roughly
crushed sugar lumps or leave plain if preferred.

pear, cardamom & sultana cake

Cuts into **10**
Preparation time **20 minutes**
Cooking time **1¼–1½ hours**

125 g (4 oz) **unsalted butter**,
  at room temperature
125 g (4 oz) **light soft brown
  sugar**
2 **eggs**, lightly beaten
250 g (8 oz) **self-raising flour**
1 teaspoon **ground
  cardamom**
4 tablespoons **milk**
500 g (1 lb) **pears**, peeled,
  cored and thinly sliced
125 g (4 oz) **sultanas**
1 tablespoon **clear honey**

Beat the butter and sugar together in a mixing bowl until pale and creamy. Gradually beat in the eggs, a little at a time, until incorporated. Sift the flour and ground cardamom together and fold them into the creamed mixture with the milk.

Reserve about one-third of the pear slices and roughly chop the rest. Fold the chopped pears into the creamed mixture with the sultanas. Spoon the mixture into a greased 1 kg (2 lb) loaf tin, its base and 2 long sides also lined with oiled greaseproof paper. Spread the surface level.

Arrange the reserved pear slices along the centre of the cake, pressing them in gently. Bake in a preheated oven, 160°C (325°F), Gas Mark 3, for 1¼–1½ hours or until a skewer inserted into the centre comes out clean.

Remove the cake from the oven. Leave to cool in the tin for 10 minutes then loosen the edges and lift out of the tin using the lining paper. Transfer to a wire rack, peel off the lining paper and leave to cool completely. Drizzle with the honey.

For date & apple ripple cake, simmer 250 g (8 oz) ready-chopped, stoned dates in a covered saucepan with 150 ml (¼ pint) water for 5 minutes until soft. Purée until smooth. Make the cake as above, but omit the cardamom, pears, sultanas and honey and replace them with 375 g (12 oz) peeled and diced cooking apples. Spoon half into the cake tin, top with the date mixture and then the remaining cake mixture. Bake as above.

spiced marmalade cake

Cuts into **24**
Preparation time **25 minutes**
Cooking time **35–40 minutes**

125 g (4 oz) **butter**
200 g (7 oz) **golden syrup**
100 g (3½ oz) **caster sugar**
2 tablespoons **chunky marmalade**
2 tablespoons **chopped candied peel** (optional)
250 g (8 oz) **self-raising flour**
2 teaspoons **ground mixed spice**
1 teaspoon **ground ginger**
½ teaspoon **bicarbonate of soda**
150 ml (¼ pint) **milk**
2 **eggs**, beaten

For the topping
2 **oranges**, thinly sliced
50 g (2 oz) **caster sugar**
200 ml (7 fl oz) **water**
2 tablespoons **marmalade**

Put the butter, golden syrup, sugar and marmalade in a saucepan and heat gently until melted.

Remove from the heat and stir in the chopped peel, if using, and the dry ingredients. Add the milk and beaten eggs and mix until smooth. Pour into a 20 cm (8 inch) deep square cake tin, greased and base-lined with oiled greaseproof paper. Bake in a preheated oven, 180°C (350°F), Gas Mark 4, for 35–40 minutes until well risen and a skewer inserted into the centre comes out clean.

Meanwhile, put the sliced oranges into a saucepan with the sugar and water. Cover and simmer for 25 minutes until tender. Remove the lid and cook for 5 minutes more, until the liquid has been reduced to about 2 tablespoons. Add the marmalade and heat until melted.

Leave the cake to cool in the tin for 10 minutes then loosen the edges, turn out on to a wire rack and peel off the lining paper. Turn the cake the right way up and spoon over the oranges and sauce. Store in an airtight tin for up to 3 days.

For light pecan gingerbread, omit the marmalade from the recipe and add 3 teaspoons ground ginger instead of the mixture of ginger and mixed spice. Stir in 40 g (1½ oz) halved pecan nuts, then pour into the cake tin and bake as above. Omit the topping.

dundee cake

Cuts into **12–14**
Preparation time **30 minutes**
Cooking time **1¾ –2 hours**

250 g (8 oz) **plain flour**
1 teaspoon **baking powder**
1 teaspoon **mixed spice**
50 g (2 oz) **ground almonds**
grated rind and juice of
    ½ **lemon**
175 g (6 oz) **butter**, at room
    temperature
175 g (6 oz) **light muscovado
    sugar**
4 **eggs**, beaten
500 g (1 lb) **luxury mixed
    dried fruit**
25 g (1 oz) **blanched
    almonds**

Mix the flour, baking powder, spice, ground almonds and lemon rind together in a bowl.

Beat the butter and sugar together in another bowl until pale and creamy. Gradually mix in alternate spoonfuls of beaten egg and flour mixture until all has been added and the mixture is smooth. Stir in the dried fruit and the lemon juice.

Spoon the mixture into a 20 cm (8 inch) deep round cake tin lined base and sides with nonstick baking paper. Spread the surface level and arrange the almonds in rings over the top. Bake in a preheated oven, 160°C (325°F), Gas Mark 3, for 1¾–2 hours until a deep brown and a skewer inserted into the centre comes out clean. Check the cake after 1 hour and cover loosely with foil if the almonds look as though they are going to overbrown.

Leave to cool in the tin for 15 minutes then loosen the edges, turn out on to a wire rack and peel off the lining paper. Leave to cool completely. Store in an airtight tin for up to 1 week.

For Easter simnel cake, make the cake mixture as above and spoon half of it into the tin and spread level. Roll out 175 g (6 oz) yellow marzipan to the same size of the tin and press onto the cake mixture. Top with the remaining cake mixture. Omit the nut topping and bake as above. To finish, brush the top of the cake with 1 tablespoon smooth apricot jam then cover with 175 g (6 oz) rolled marzipan to fit the top. Crimp the edges and brown lightly under the grill.

tropical christmas cake

Cuts into **10**
Preparation time **30 minutes**
Cooking time **1¼–1½ hours**

300 g (10 oz) **unsalted
    butter**, at room temperature
200 g (7 oz) **caster sugar**
3 large **eggs**, beaten
425 g (14 oz) **self-raising
    flour**, sifted
75 g (3 oz) **glacé cherries**,
50 g (2 oz) **mixed peel**
3 tablespoons **angelica**
3 tablespoons **walnuts**
250 g (8 oz) can **pineapple
    rings in syrup**, drained and
    the syrup reserved
3 tablespoons **desiccated
    coconut**
75 g (3 oz) **sultanas**
2 tablespoons toasted
    coconut shavings,
    to decorate

For the icing
250 g (8 oz) **icing sugar**
40 g (1½ oz) **unsalted butter**,
    melted
2 tablespoons **desiccated
    coconut**

Beat the butter and sugar together in a bowl until pale and creamy. Gradually mix in alternate spoonfuls of beaten egg and flour until all has been added.

Chop the dried fruit, nuts and pineapple and then fold into the cake mixture with the coconut, sultanas and 3 tablespoons of the reserved pineapple syrup.

Spoon the mixture into a greased and floured 23 cm (9 inch) ring mould or 20 cm (8 inch) cake tin. Bake in a preheated oven, 160°C (325°F), Gas Mark 3, for 1¼ hours if using a ring mould and 1½ hours if using a cake tin. Leave to cool in the tin for at least 10 minutes then loosen the edges and turn out on to a wire rack. Leave to cool completely.

Make the icing. Sift the icing sugar into the melted butter, then add 1 tablespoon of the reserved pineapple syrup and the coconut. Stir to combine, then spread the icing over the top of the cake and a little down the sides. Sprinkle with toasted coconut shavings to decorate.

For paradise cake, replace the pineapple juice with 3 tablespoons dark rum in the cake mixture and continue as above. Decorate the top of the cooked cake with a rich, dark chocolate frosting made by heating 2 tablespoons butter and 125 g (4 oz) dark chocolate gently in a pan. Mix in 3 tablespoons icing sugar and 2–3 teaspoons milk to make a smooth spoonable frosting. Spoon over the top of the cake and decorate with extra angelica and glacé cherries.

198

cranberry & cherry cake

Cuts into **12**
Preparation time **30 minutes**
Cooking time **1 hour 10 minutes–1 hour 20 minutes**

200 g (7 oz) **glacé cherries**
175 g (6 oz) **butter**, at room temperature
175 g (6 oz) **caster sugar**
grated rind of 1 small **orange**
3 **eggs**, beaten
225 g (7½ oz) **self-raising flour**
50 g (2 oz) **dried cranberries**
a few **sugar lumps**, roughly crushed, to decorate

Put the cherries in a sieve, rinse with cold water then drain and pat dry with kitchen paper. (This ensures they don't sink during cooking.) Halve 50 g (2 oz) and reserve for decoration. Roughly chop the remainder.

Beat the butter and sugar together in a mixing bowl or a food processor until pale and creamy. Stir in the orange rind then gradually mix in alternate spoonfuls of beaten egg and flour until all has been added and the mixture is smooth.

Fold in the chopped glacé cherries and cranberries. Spoon the mixture into an 18 cm (7 inch) deep round cake tin lined base and sides with nonstick baking paper. Spread the surface level then lightly press the reserved halved cherries into the cake mixture and sprinkle with the crushed sugar lumps.

Bake in a preheated oven, 160°C (325°F), Gas Mark 3, for about 1 hour 10 minutes–1 hour 20 minutes until well risen, the top is golden brown and a skewer inserted into the centre comes out clean.

Leave to cool in the tin for 10 minutes then loosen the edges, turn out on to a wire rack and peel off the lining paper. Leave to cool completely. Store in an airtight tin for up to 5 days.

For date & apricot cake, omit the cherries and cranberries and add 125 g (4 oz) roughly chopped stoned dates and 125 g (4 oz) chopped ready-to-eat dried apricots. Bake as above, leaving the top of the cake plain.

lemon & poppy seed cake

Cuts into **10**
Preparation time **25 minutes**
Cooking time **1 hour–1 hour
 10 minutes**

175 g (6 oz) **butter**, at room
 temperature
175 g (6 oz) **caster sugar**
3 **eggs**, beaten
250 g (8 oz) **self-raising flour**
1 teaspoon **baking powder**
40 g (1½ oz) **poppy seeds**
grated rind and juice of 2
 lemons

To finish
125 g (4 oz) **icing sugar**
3–4 teaspoons **lemon juice**
citron peel, cut into thin strips

Beat the butter and sugar together in a mixing bowl until pale and creamy. Gradually mix in alternate spoonfuls of beaten egg and flour until all has been added and the mixture is smooth. Stir in the baking powder, poppy seeds, lemon rind and 5–6 tablespoons lemon juice to make a soft dropping consistency.

Spoon the mixture into a greased 1 kg (2 lb) loaf tin, its base and 2 long sides also lined with oiled greaseproof paper. Spread the surface level and bake in a preheated oven, 160°C (325°F), Gas Mark 3, for 1 hour–1 hour 10 minutes until well risen, the top is cracked and golden and a skewer inserted into the centre comes out clean.

Leave to cool in the tin for 10 minutes then loosen the edges and lift out of the tin using the lining paper. Transfer to a wire rack, peel off the lining paper and leave to cool.

Sift the icing sugar into a bowl then gradually mix in enough of the lemon juice to make a smooth coating icing. Drizzle over the top of the cake in random squiggly lines. Add strips of peel to the top and leave to set. Store in an airtight tin for up to 1 week.

For orange & caraway cake, follow the recipe above but replace the poppy seeds and lemon with 1½ teaspoons roughly crushed caraway seeds, the grated rind of 1 large orange and 5–6 tablespoons orange juice. Decorate the top of the cake with 25 g (1 oz) roughly crushed sugar lumps before baking and omit the lemon icing.

apricot tea bread

Cuts into **10**

Preparation time **25 minutes, plus soaking**

Cooking time **1 hour**

100 g (3½ oz) **ready-to-eat dried apricots**, chopped
100 g (3½ oz) **sultanas**
100 g (3½ oz) **raisins**
150 g (5 oz) **caster sugar**
300 ml (½ pint) **hot strong tea**
275 g (9 oz) **self-raising flour**
1 teaspoon **bicarbonate of soda**
1 teaspoon **ground cinnamon**
1 **egg**, beaten

Put the dried fruits and sugar in a mixing bowl, add the hot tea and mix together. Leave to soak for 4 hours or overnight.

Mix the flour, bicarbonate of soda and cinnamon together, add to the soaked fruit with the beaten egg and mix together well.

Spoon into a greased 1 kg (2 lb) loaf tin, its base and 2 long sides also lined with oiled greaseproof paper. Spread the surface level then bake in the centre of a preheated oven, 160°C (325°F), Gas Mark 3, for about 1 hour until well risen, the top has cracked and a skewer inserted into the centre comes out clean.

Leave to cool in the tin for 10 minutes then loosen the edges and lift out of the tin using the lining paper. Transfer to a wire rack, peel off the lining paper and leave to cool completely. Cut into slices and spread with a little butter to serve. Store, unbuttered, in an airtight tin for up to 1 week.

For prune & orange bread, use 175 g (6 oz) chopped ready-to-eat stoned prunes instead of the apricots and sultanas, and increase the quantity of raisins to 125 g (4 oz). Mix with the caster sugar as above, add the grated rind of 1 orange, then soak in 150 ml (¼ pint) orange juice and 150 ml (¼ pint) boiling water instead of the tea. Add the flour, bicarbonate of soda and beaten egg as above, omitting the cinnamon. Spoon into a loaf tin and continue the recipe as above.

pastries

citrus baklava

Makes **24**
Preparation time **30 minutes, plus chilling**
Cooking time **35–40 minutes**

400 g (13 oz) packet **frozen filo pastry**, defrosted
125 g (4 oz) **butter**, melted

For the filling
100 g (3½ oz) **walnut pieces**
100 g (3½ oz) **shelled pistachio nuts**
100 g (3½ oz) **blanched almonds**
75 g (3 oz) **caster sugar**
½ teaspoon **ground cinnamon**

For the syrup
1 **lemon**
1 small **orange**
250 g (8 oz) **caster sugar**
pinch of **ground cinnamon**
150 ml (¼ pint) **water**

To decorate
few slivers **pistachio nuts**

Dry-fry the nuts in a nonstick pan for 3–4 minutes, stirring until lightly browned. Leave to cool slightly then roughly chop and mix with the sugar and spice.

Unfold the pastry and cut it into rectangles the same size as the base of an 18 x 28 cm (7 x 11 inch) small roasting tin. Wrap half the pastry in clingfilm so that it doesn't dry out. Brush each unwrapped sheet of pastry with melted butter then layer up in the roasting tin. Spoon in the nut mixture then unwrap and cover with the remaining pastry, buttering layers as you go.

Cut the pastry into 6 squares, then cut each square into 4 triangles. Bake in a preheated oven, 180°C (350°F), Gas Mark 4, for 30–35 minutes, covering with foil after 20 minutes to prevent it overbrowning.

Meanwhile, make the syrup. Pare the rind off the citrus fruits with a zester or vegetable peeler then cut the rind into strips. Squeeze the juice. Put the strips and juice in a saucepan with the sugar, cinnamon and water. Heat gently until the sugar dissolves then simmer for 5 minutes without stirring.

Pour the hot syrup over the pastry as soon as it comes out of the oven. Leave to cool, then chill for 3 hours. Remove from the tin and arrange the pieces on a serving plate, sprinkled with slivers of pistachio. Store in the refrigerator for up to 2 days.

For rose water baklava, omit the orange rind and juice from the syrup and add 4 tablespoons extra water and 1 tablespoon rose water, or to taste. Pour over the cooked baklava and finish as above.

french apple flan

Makes **4**

Preparation time **20 minutes, plus chilling**

Cooking time **25–30 minutes**

375 g (12 oz) **ready-made puff pastry**

2 **crisp green dessert apples** (such as Granny Smith), peeled, cored and sliced

1 tablespoon **caster sugar**

25 g (1 oz) **unsalted butter**, chilled

crème fraîche, to serve

For the apricot glaze

250 g (8 oz) **apricot jam**

2 teaspoons **lemon juice**

2 teaspoons **water**

Divide the pastry into quarters and roll each out on a lightly floured surface until 2 mm (⅛ inch) thick. Using a 13 cm (5½ inch) plate as a guide, cut out 4 rounds – make a number of short cuts around the plate rather than drawing the knife around, which can stretch the pastry. Place the rounds on a baking sheet.

Place a slightly smaller plate on each pastry round and score around the edge to form a 1 cm (½ inch) border. Prick the centres with a fork and chill for 30 minutes.

Arrange the apple slices in a circle over the pastry rounds and sprinkle with the sugar. Grate the butter over the top and bake in a preheated oven, 220°C (425°F), Gas Mark 7, for 25–30 minutes until the pastry and apples are golden.

Meanwhile, make the apricot glaze. Put the jam in a small saucepan with the lemon juice and water and heat gently until the jam melts. Increase the heat and boil for 1 minute, remove from the heat and press through a fine sieve. Keep warm then brush over each apple tart while they are still warm. Serve with ice cream.

For peach tartlets, replace the 2 apples with 2 peaches, halved, skinned and thinly sliced. Arrange on the pastry rounds and continue as above, baking for 12–15 minutes.

chocolate éclairs with cream liqueur

Makes **18**
Preparation time **40 minutes,
  plus cooling**
Cooking time **15 minutes**

150 ml (¼ pint) **water**
50 g (2 oz) **butter**
65 g (2½ oz) **plain flour**, sifted
2 **eggs**, beaten
½ teaspoon **vanilla essence**

For the filling
250 ml (8 fl oz) **double cream**
2 tablespoons **icing sugar**
4 tablespoons **whisky and
  coffee cream liqueur** (such
  as Baileys)

For the topping
25 g (1 oz) **butter**
100 g (3½ oz) **plain dark
  chocolate**, broken into
  pieces
1 tablespoon **icing sugar**
2–3 teaspoons **milk**

Heat the water and butter gently in a saucepan until melted. Bring to the boil then add the flour and beat until it forms a smooth ball that leaves the sides of the pan almost clean. Leave to cool for 10 minutes.

Gradually mix in the eggs and vanilla until thick and smooth. Spoon the choux mixture into a large nylon piping bag fitted with a 1 cm (½ inch) plain piping tube and pipe 7.5 cm (3 inch) lines of mixture on to a large lightly greased baking sheet.

Bake in a preheated oven, 200°C (400°F), Gas Mark 6, for 15 minutes until well risen. Make a slit in the side of each éclair for the steam to escape then return to the turned-off oven for 5 minutes. Leave to cool.

Whip the cream to soft swirls then gradually whisk in the icing sugar and liqueur. Slit each éclair lengthways and spoon or pipe in the cream.

Make the chocolate topping. Heat the butter, chocolate and icing sugar together gently until just melted. Stir in the milk then spoon over the top of the éclairs. Serve the same day.

For chocolate profiteroles, pipe small balls of the choux mixture on to baking sheets. Bake as above for 10–12 minutes. When cool, fill with plain whipped cream and drizzle with a smooth chocolate sauce made by gently heating 150 g (5 oz) plain dark chocolate with 15 g (½ oz) butter, 25 g (1 oz) caster sugar and 150 ml (¼ pint) milk.

raspberry garlands

Makes **8**
Preparation time **30 minutes,
plus cooling**
Cooking time **15 minutes**

150 ml (¼ pint) **water**
50 g (2 oz) **butter**
65 g (2½ oz) **plain flour**, sifted
2 **eggs**, beaten
½ teaspoon **vanilla essence**
15 g (½ oz) **flaked almonds**
sifted **icing sugar**, for dusting

For the filling
300 ml (½ pint) **full-fat crème
fraîche**
3 tablespoons **icing sugar**,
sifted
250 g (8 oz) **fresh raspberries**

Heat the water and butter gently in a saucepan until melted. Bring to the boil then add the flour and beat until it forms a smooth ball that leaves the sides of the pan almost clean. Leave to cool for 10 minutes.

Gradually mix in the eggs and vanilla until thick and smooth. Spoon the choux mixture into a large nylon piping bag fitted with a 1 cm (½ inch) plain piping tube and pipe 7.5 cm (3 inch) diameter circles on a greased baking sheet.

Sprinkle with the flaked almonds then bake in a preheated oven, 200°C (400°F), Gas Mark 6, for 15 minutes. Make a small slit in the side of each choux ring for the steam to escape then return to the turned-off oven for 5 minutes. Leave to cool.

Slit each choux ring and fill with crème fraîche mixed with half the icing sugar then sprinkle with the raspberries. Arrange on a serving plate and dust with the remaining icing sugar. These are best eaten on the day they are made.

For strawberry cream puffs, make the choux pastry as above and pipe 8 choux balls on to a greased baking sheet. Bake as above until crisp then fill the puffs with 150 g (5 oz) fromage frais mixed with 150 ml (¼ pint) whipped double cream sweetened with 2 tablespoons icing sugar and 250 g (8 oz) sliced strawberries. Dust the tops with sifted icing sugar.

baby banana & peach strudels

Makes **8**
Preparation time **30 minutes**
Cooking time **15–18 minutes**

2 **bananas**, about 175 g
  (6 oz) each with skin on,
  peeled and chopped
2 tablespoons fresh **lemon
  juice**
2 small **ripe peaches**, about
  100 g (3½ oz) each, halved,
  stoned and sliced
100 g (3½ oz) **blueberries**
2 tablespoons **caster sugar**
2 tablespoons **fresh
  breadcrumbs**
½ teaspoon **ground cinnamon**
270 g (9 oz) packet 6 **filo
  pastry sheets**, defrosted if
  frozen
50 g (2 oz) **butter**, melted
sifted **icing sugar**, for dusting

Toss the bananas in the lemon juice then place in a large bowl with the peach slices and blueberries. Mix the sugar, breadcrumbs and cinnamon in a small bowl then gently mix with the fruit.

Unfold the pastry sheets, put one in front of you with the longest edge nearest you.

Cut in half to make 2 rectangles, 23 x 25 cm (9 x 10 inches). Put 2 heaped spoonfuls of the fruit mixture on each then fold in the sides, brush the pastry with a little of the melted butter then roll up like a parcel. Repeat to make 8 mini strudels using 4 sheets of pastry.

Brush the strudels with a little more melted butter. Cut the remaining pastry sheets into wide strips then wrap them like bandages around the strudels, covering any tears or splits in the pastry. Place on an ungreased baking sheet and brush with the remaining butter.

Bake in a preheated oven, 190°C (375°F), Gas Mark 5, for 15–18 minutes until golden brown and crisp. Leave to cool on the baking sheet then dust with a little sifted icing sugar and arrange on a serving plate. These are best eaten on the day they are made.

For traditional apple strudels, replace the bananas and peaches with 500 g (1 lb) cored, peeled and sliced cooking apples tossed with 2 tablespoons lemon juice and mixed with 50 g (2 oz) sultanas. Use ground almonds instead of the breadcrumbs and combine with the cinnamon. Increase the quantity of sugar to 50 g (2 oz) and continue the recipe as above.

classic lemon tart

Cuts into **8**
Preparation time **20 minutes,
plus chilling**
Cooking time **40–45 minutes**

200 g (7 oz) **plain flour**
½ teaspoon **salt**
100 g (3½ oz) **butter**, diced
2 tablespoons **icing sugar**,
plus extra for dusting
2 **egg yolks**
1–2 teaspoons **cold water**

For the filling
3 **eggs**, plus 1 **egg yolk**
475 ml (16 fl oz) **double
cream**
100 g (3½ oz) **sugar**
150 ml (¼ pint) **lemon juice**

Put the flour and salt in a mixing bowl. Add the butter and rub in with your fingertips until the mixture resembles fine breadcrumbs.

Stir in the icing sugar and gradually work in the egg yolks and water to make a firm dough.

Knead the dough briefly on a lightly floured surface, then cover with clingfilm and chill for 30 minutes. Roll out the dough and use to line a 25 cm (10 inch) fluted pie dish or tart tin. Prick the pastry case with a fork and chill for 20 minutes.

Line the pastry case with baking paper and ceramic baking beans and bake in a preheated oven, 200°C (400°F), Gas Mark 6, for 10 minutes. Remove the paper and beans and bake for a further 10 minutes until crisp and golden. Remove from the oven and reduce the temperature to 150°C (300°F), Gas Mark 2.

Beat together all the filling ingredients, pour them into the pastry case, and bake for 20–25 minutes, or until the filling is just set. Let the tart cool completely, dust with sifted icing sugar and serve.

For dark chocolate tart, make the tart base as above and bake blind. Heat 450 ml (¾ pint) double cream in a saucepan with 150 g (5 oz) dark chocolate, stirring until the chocolate has melted. Whisk 3 eggs and 1 egg yolk with 50 g (2 oz) caster sugar and ¼ teaspoon ground cinnamon. Gradually whisk in the chocolate cream. Bake as above and serve cold, dusted with sifted cocoa powder.

custard cream berry slices

Makes **8**
Preparation time **40 minutes**
Cooking time **13–16 minutes**

375 g (12 oz) packet **frozen puff pastry**, defrosted
250 ml (8 fl oz) **double cream**
150 g (5 oz) carton **ready-made custard**
200 g (7 oz) **strawberries**, sliced
150 g (5 oz) **raspberries**
icing sugar, sifted, optional

Roll out the pastry on a lightly floured surface and cut into 2 strips, 10 x 30 cm (4 x 12 inches). Space apart on a wetted baking sheet. Prick with a fork and bake in a preheated oven, 220°C (425°F), Gas Mark 7, for 10–12 minutes until well risen.

Slice each strip in half horizontally, lift off the tops and place, baked side downwards, on a separate baking sheet. Bake all strips for 3–4 minutes more to dry out the soft centres. Leave to cool.

Whip the cream then fold in the custard and spoon over 3 of the pastry strips. Arrange the strawberries and raspberries on top of each strip and then assemble. Add the last pastry slice, if liked and dust with icing sugar. Transfer to a large serving plate. Cut each custard slice into 4 to serve. These are best eaten on the day they are made.

For coffee cream slices, cook the pastry as above. Dissolve 3 teaspoons instant coffee in 2 teaspoons boiling water. Stir into the cream and custard mix. Use to sandwich the pastry strips together, omitting the summer berries. Add the fourth pastry layer and drizzle with the topping from the Chocolate éclairs with cream liqueur on page 212, and a few chocolate curls to decorate.

no-bake
cakes

cheat's lemon dainties

Cuts into **9**
Preparation time **25 minutes,
plus chilling**

8 **trifle sponges**, sliced in half
horizontally to give shallower
pieces
100 g (3½ oz) **butter**,
at room temperature
100 g (3½ oz) **caster sugar**
grated rind of 2 **lemons**
2 **eggs**, separated
150 ml (¼ pint) **double cream**
juice of 1 **lemon**

To finish
4 tablespoons **icing sugar**
125 g (4 oz) **fresh raspberries**
100 g (3½ oz) **blueberries**
fresh mint leaves

Line a 20 cm (8 inch) shallow square cake tin with
clingfilm. Arrange half of the trifle sponges in a single
layer in the base of the tin.

Beat the butter, sugar and lemon rind together until
pale and creamy. Gradually whisk in the egg yolks.

Whisk the egg whites in a large clean bowl until stiff,
then whip the cream in a separate bowl. Fold the
whipped cream then the egg whites into the creamed
mixture. Gradually fold in the juice of ½ lemon.

Drizzle a little of the remaining lemon juice over the
trifle sponges. Spoon the cream mixture on top and
gently spread the surface level. Cover with a second
layer of sponge slices, press them gently into the
cream mixture and drizzle with the remaining lemon
juice. Cover with an extra piece of clingfilm and chill
in the refrigerator for 4 hours or overnight.

Remove the top layer of clingfilm, invert the cake on
to a chopping board and peel off the remaining
clingfilm. Decorate with berries and mint leaves,
dusting the tops with icing sugar. Eat within 2 days of
making, store in the refrigerator.

For tiramisu squares, mix 4 tablespoons strong
black coffee with 2 tablespoons sherry. Spoon half
over the trifle sponges in the tin. Beat 250 g (8 oz)
mascarpone cheese with 50 g (2 oz) caster sugar
and 150 ml (¼ pint) double cream. Spoon half into
the tin, sprinkle with 50 g (2 oz) chopped dark
chocolate, then repeat the layering with the rest of
the ingredients and the same amount of chocolate
sprinkled over the top. Chill before serving.

sicilian cheesecake

Cuts into **8**

Preparation time **20 minutes, plus chilling**

250 g (8 oz) **ricotta cheese**
50 g (2 oz) **icing sugar** (no need to sift)
150 ml (¼ pint) **double cream**
100 g (3½ oz) **plain dark chocolate**, finely chopped
75 g (3 oz) **ready-to-eat dried apricots**, finely chopped
75 g (3 oz) **multi-coloured glacé cherries**, roughly chopped
2 tablespoons **chopped candied peel**
10 **trifle sponges**
6 tablespoons **white rum**
cocoa powder, to decorate

Mix the ricotta cheese with the icing sugar. Whip the cream until it forms soft swirls then fold into the ricotta. Reserve a few pieces of the chopped chocolate, apricots, cherries and candied peel and fold the rest into the ricotta mixture.

Line an 18 cm (7 inch) deep round cake tin with 2 pieces of clingfilm so that the base and sides are covered. Arrange half the trifle sponges over the base of the cake tin, trimming to fit. Moisten with half the rum.

Spoon two-thirds of the ricotta mixture over the sponges and spread the surface level. Cover with the remaining trifle sponges and moisten with the remaining rum. Spread the rest of the ricotta mixture on top and sprinkle with the reserved chocolate and fruits, dust with cocoa powder. Chill for 4 hours or overnight.

Loosen the edges and lift the cake out of the tin using the clingfilm. Peel off the film and transfer to a serving plate. Cut into thin wedges to serve. Store in the refrigerator for up to 2 days.

For cherry kirsch gâteau, line the clingfilm-lined tin with trifle sponges but soak them in kirsch rather than rum. Top with a sweetened mascarpone cheese cream, rather than a ricotta cheese mixture, speckled with chopped chocolate, as above, plus a 425 g (14 oz) can stoned black cherries, drained and roughly chopped, instead of the dried fruit.

layered nutty bars

Cuts into **10**
Preparation time **20 minutes,
plus chilling**
Cooking time **5 minutes**

50 g (2 oz) **butter**
400 g (13 oz) **fat-free
sweetened condensed milk**
200 g (7 oz) **plain dark
chocolate**, broken into
pieces
125 g (4 oz) **rich tea biscuits**
50 g (2 oz) **hazelnuts**
100 g (3½ oz) **shelled
pistachio nuts**

Use a little of the butter to grease the base and sides of a 20 cm (8 inch) round spring-form tin. Put the rest of the butter in a saucepan with the condensed milk and chocolate. Heat gently for 3–4 minutes, stirring until melted, then remove from the heat.

Place the biscuits in a plastic bag and crush roughly into chunky pieces using a rolling pin. Toast the hazelnuts under a preheated hot grill until lightly browned, then roughly chop with the pistachios.

Stir the biscuits into the chocolate mixture then spoon half the mixture into the prepared tin and spread level. Reserve 2 tablespoons of the nuts for the top, then sprinkle the rest over the chocolate biscuit layer. Cover with the remaining chocolate mixture, level the surface with the back of the spoon and sprinkle with the reserved nuts.

Chill the nut mixture for 3–4 hours until firm, then loosen the edges and remove the sides of the tin. Cut into 10 thin slices, or into tiny bite-sized pieces to make petits fours. Store any leftovers in the refrigerator, wrapped in foil, for up to 3 days.

For gingered fruit bars, make the chocolate mix as above and stir in crushed digestive biscuits instead of the rich tea biscuits. Omit the nuts and use 50 g (2 oz) roughly chopped ready-to-eat dried apricots and 2 tablespoons chopped glacé ginger, keeping 2–3 tablespoons back for the topping.

diplomatico

Cuts into **8**
Preparation time **25 minutes,**
 plus chilling

200 g (7 oz) **plain dark**
 chocolate, broken into
 pieces
300 ml (½ pint) **double cream**
3 tablespoons **icing sugar**
 (no need to sift)
4 tablespoons **brandy** or
 coffee liqueur
100 ml (3½ fl oz) **strong black**
 coffee, cooled
30 **sponge finger biscuits**

To decorate
150 ml (¼ pint) **double cream**
cocoa powder, sifted

Melt the chocolate in a heatproof bowl set over a saucepan of gently simmering water. Meanwhile, line a 1 kg (2 lb) loaf tin with clingfilm so that the base and sides are covered.

Whip the cream until softly peaking. Fold in the icing sugar then the melted chocolate. Spoon a thin layer into the base of the lined tin.

Mix the brandy or coffee liqueur and cooled coffee in a shallow dish. Dip the sponge finger biscuits, one at a time, into the mixture to moisten then arrange in a single layer on top of the chocolate cream in the tin. Cover with half the remaining cream, then a second layer of dipped biscuits. Repeat the layers until all the cream and biscuits have been used.

Chill for 4 hours or overnight if preferred. To serve, loosen the edges and invert on to a serving plate. Peel off the clingfilm. Whip the double cream and spoon over the top, then dust with cocoa powder. Cut into thick slices to serve. Refrigerate for up to 2 days.

For tiramisu, sweeten 250 g (8 oz) mascarpone cheese with 2 tablespoons icing sugar and mix with 150 ml (¼ pint) whipped double cream. Layer in the clingfilm-lined loaf tin as above with coffee liqueur and coffee-dipped biscuits. Decorate with chocolate curls.

chocolate yum yums

Cuts into **15**

Preparation time **15 minutes, plus chilling**

150 g (5 oz) **plain dark chocolate**, broken into pieces

100 g (3½ oz) **crunchy peanut butter**

25 g (1 oz) **butter**

2 tablespoons **golden syrup**

150 g (5 oz) **digestive biscuits**

50 g (2 oz) **almonds or cashew nuts**

sugared almonds, roughly chopped, to decorate

Put the chocolate, peanut butter, butter and syrup in a saucepan and heat gently until melted, stirring occasionally. Remove from the heat.

Place the biscuits in a plastic bag and crush roughly using a rolling pin. Stir the crushed biscuits and the nuts into the chocolate and stir until evenly coated.

Spoon the mixture into a 20 cm (8 inch) shallow square cake tin lined with nonstick baking paper, and spread the surface level. Chill for 4 hours until firm. Lift the cake out of the tin using the lining paper, cut into 15 small squares and peel off the paper. Decorate with sugared almonds. Store in an airtight tin for up to 3 days.

For chocolate marshmallow wedges, omit the peanut butter, nuts and sugared almonds. Melt the chocolate with 75 g (3 oz) butter and 75 g (3 oz) golden syrup. Cool slightly then stir in 65 g (2½ oz) roughly chopped sponge fingers, 65 g (2½ oz) roughly chopped glacé cherries and 100 g (3½ oz) mini marshmallows. Spoon into a clingfilm-lined 20 cm (8 inch) round tin and sprinkle the top with 25 g (1 oz) halved mini marshmallows. Chill as above. Remove from the tin, peel off the clingfilm and cut into thin wedges.

cornflake crunchies

Makes **20**
Preparation time **15 minutes,
   plus chilling**

200 g (7 oz) **plain dark
   chocolate**, broken into
   pieces
50 g (2 oz) **butter**
3 tablespoons **golden syrup**
125 g (4 oz) **cornflakes**
mini marshmallows, sliced,
   to decorate

Place the chocolate in a saucepan with the butter and golden syrup. Heat gently, stirring occasionally, until the chocolate and butter have completely melted and the mixture is smooth and glossy.

Stir in the cornflakes and mix until completely coated in the chocolate. Spoon the cornflake mixture into 20 paper cake cases arranged on a tray or baking sheet and chill for 2–3 hours until firm. Decorate with sliced mini marshmallows.

For chocolate orange crispie cakes, follow the recipe above but replace the cornflakes with the same weight of puffed rice cereal and adding the grated rind of 1 small orange. Finish as above.

index

acknowledgements

Executive Editor: Nicola Hill
Editor: Ruth Wiseall
Executive Art Editor: Darren Southern
Designer: Martin Topping 'ome Design
Photographer: William Shaw
Home Economist: Sara Lewis
Food and Props Stylist: Liz Hippisley
Senior Production Controller: Manjit Sihra

Special photography: © Octopus Publishing
  Group Ltd/William Shaw.
Other photography: © Octopus Publishing
  Group Ltd/Stephen Conroy 19, 69, 145;
  /William Lingwood 25, 41, 61, 85, 93, 97, 157,
  161, 165, 177, 179, 193, 211; /Emma Neish
  133, 139, 171; /Lis Parsons 33, 73, 77, 81, 89,
  149, 199, 219, 229; /Gareth Sambidge 103;
  /Ian Wallace 141, 175.